The Environment of
Schizophrenia

Innova
and co

Richa

London

First published 2000
by Brunner-Routledge
11 New Fetter Lane, London EC4P 4EE

Simultaneously published in the USA and Canada
by Taylor & Francis Inc
325 Chestnut Street, 8th Floor, Philadelphia PA 19106

Brunner-Routledge is an imprint of the Taylor & Francis Group

© 2000 Richard Warner

Typeset in Times by
Keystroke, Jacaranda Lodge, Wolverhampton
Printed and bound in Great Britain by
TJ International Ltd, Padstow, Cornwall

British Library Cataloguing in Publication Data
A catalogue record for this book is available from the British Library

Library of Congress Cataloging in Publication Data
Warner, Richard, 1943–
    The environment of schizophrenia / Richard Warner.
        p. cm.
    1. Schizophrenia–Environmental aspects. 2. Schizophrenia–Treatment.
    3. Schizophrenics–Rehabilitation. I. Title.

RC514 .W238 2000
616.89′82–dc21   00–032843

ISBN 0–415–22306–7 (hbk)
ISBN 0–415–22307–5 (pbk)

The Environment of Schizophrenia

There is now a body of evidence suggesting that the occurrence and course of schizophrenia are affected by a variety of environmental factors. *The Environment of Schizophrenia* draws upon our knowledge of these factors in order to design innovations that will decrease its incidence and severity, while enhancing the quality of life for sufferers and their relatives.

Examining environmental forces operating at the individual, domestic and broad societal levels, Richard Warner proposes feasible interventions such as:

- education about obstetric risks
- marketing effective psychosocial treatments
- business enterprises set up to employ people with mental illness
- cognitive-behavioral therapy for psychosis

The Environment of Schizophrenia suggests practical ways to create a better world for those who suffer from this serious illness and for those who are close to them. It will prove fresh and stimulating reading for mental health service managers and policy makers, as well as psychiatrists, clinical psychologists, mental health advocates and communications specialists.

Richard Warner is the Medical Director of the Mental Health Center of Boulder County, Colorado, and Clinical Professor of Psychiatry and Adjunct Professor of Anthropology at the University of Colorado. He is the author of *Recovery from Schizophrenia* (Routledge, 1994) and numerous other publications on the epidemiology and community treatment of schizophrenia.

To those who suffer from schizophrenia
and those who suffer, struggle,
and rejoice in successes alongside them

Contents

Figures and tables

Figures

Tables

Acknowledgements

I am very grateful for the help provided by many of my friends and associates in the preparation of this book and in conducting the research and the projects which are mentioned here. Among them are Mona Wasow, at the School of Social Work at the University of Wisconsin in Madison, who came up with the idea of writing up one's pipe-dreams – "speculative innovations" as she called them; Paul Polak at International Development Enterprises in Lakewood, Colorado, Julian Leff and Peter Huxley at the Institute of Psychiatry in London, and Jim Mandiberg at the School of Social Work of the University of Wisconsin in Madison, who helped work out many of the ideas presented here; Dawn Taylor and David Miklowitz of the University of Colorado Department of Psychology in Boulder, and Paul Polak, who were collaborators on a variety of research projects cited here; Giovanni de Girolamo at the National Institute of Health in Rome, Angelo Fioritti with the Mental Health Service in Bologna, and Sofia Piccione at the University of Bologna, who were collaborators in cross-national research; my many colleagues, including Phoebe Norton and Charlotte Wollesen, at the Mental Health Center of Boulder County in Colorado, who helped design and operate the treatment programs described here; Sue Estroff in the School of Medicine at the University of Northern Carolina in Chapel Hill, who was helpful in sharing her knowledge of consumer organizations, as was Peter Huxley at the Institute of Psychiatry in London and Ron Coleman with the Mental Health Network in Birmingham, England; Robert Freedman at the University of Colorado Department of Psychiatry in Denver, who helped keep me abreast of the latest biological research in schizophrenia; Gary Bond at Indiana-Purdue University in Indianapolis, who brought me up to date on recent outcome research on psychosocial interventions; Norman Sartorius, of the World Psychiatric Association, and Hugh Schulze of Closer Look Creative Inc. in Chicago, who are among the prime movers in the World Psychiatric Association global anti-stigma campaign; Julio Arboleda-Florez and Heather Stuart at Queen's University in Kingston, Ontario, Ruth Dickson at Calgary General Hospital, Fay Herrick in the Schizophrenia Society and the many other people in Calgary, Alberta, who volunteered their time for the anti-stigma campaign in Calgary; and Marilyn Rothman, the dazzling research librarian at the Mental Health Center of Boulder County. The book would not have been possible without the help of these and many others; the faults, needless to say, are all mine.

I am especially indebted to my wife, Lucy Warner, for her advice, support and patience.

Figure I.3 is taken from Gottesman, I.I., *Schizophrenia Genesis: The Origins of Madness*, New York, W.H. Freeman, 1991, p. 96, © 1991 Irving I. Gottesman, by permission of the author. The themes of this book were previously developed in various publications including Warner, R., "Environmental interventions in schizophrenia: 1. The individual and domestic levels" and "Environmental interventions in schizophrenia: 2. The community level," *New Directions for Mental Health*, 83, 61–84, 1999, © 1999 Jossey-Bass, and in Warner, R., "Schizophrenia and the environment: speculative interventions," *Epidemiologia e Psichiatria Sociale*, 8, 19–34, 1999, © 1999 Il Pensiero Scientifico Editore. Material in the Introduction and Chapter 3 has previously been published in Warner, R., *Recovery from Schizophrenia: Psychiatry and Political Economy*, London, Routledge, 1994, © 1994 Richard Warner; and some of the material in Chapter 7 was previously used in Warner, R., *Alternatives to the Hospital for Acute Psychiatric Treatment*, Washington, DC, American Psychiatric Press, 1996, © 1995 Richard Warner.

Introduction
What is schizophrenia?

In the title of this book, *The Environment of Schizophrenia*, the term "environment" is intended to encompass everything that affects the condition except the innate genetic predisposition. Covering every aspect of life from physical influences in the womb to the stigma and discrimination that sufferers encounter in society, it is indeed a broad field.

We can use the well-accepted bio-psycho-social model (Bloom, 1988) to clarify how different factors shape schizophrenia or any other illness. This model shows us that the predisposition to developing an illness, its onset and its course are each influenced by biological, psychological and sociocultural factors. Figure I.1 illustrates how a variety of factors can affect the various phases of schizophrenia. Most of these influences are environmental; few – only genetics, gender and synaptic pruning (see below) – are innate. Biological, psychological and social factors are involved to some extent in most phases of schizophrenia. In general, however, in schizophrenia as in other illnesses, the research suggests that the factors responsible for the predisposition to developing the illness are more likely to be biological, that psychological factors are often important in triggering the onset of a disorder, and that the course and outcome of an illness are particularly likely to be influenced by sociocultural factors (Bloom, 1985).

The aim of the book

The aim of this book is to draw upon our knowledge of the environmental factors that affect schizophrenia in order to suggest changes which could decrease the rate of occurrence of the illness, improve its course and enhance the quality of life of sufferers and their relatives. Ranging from education about obstetric risks through changes in disability pension provisions to a stigma-reducing campaign, these suggestions will be of

Phase of illness

Factor		Predisposition	Onset	Course
	Biological	e.g. obstetric complications; genetics; gender		
	Psychological		e.g. reaction to stress	
	Sociocultural			e.g. living with family; stigma

Figure 1.1 The bio-psycho-social model of schizophrenia

interest, not only to clinicians, but also to advocates, policy makers, and communications specialists.

Many, if not most, of the suggested interventions will appear novel to readers in the United States and Britain. All are feasible; in fact some are already features of the mental health system in one country or another. For example, the proposed disability pension mechanisms and family support payments are similar to those in place in Italy, cognitive-behavioural therapy for psychosis is gaining credibility in Britain, and domestic alternatives to hospital for acute psychiatric treatment are becoming more common, particularly in the United States.

What is schizophrenia?

In order to place these suggestions in perspective we should first be clear about what is meant by the term "schizophrenia."

In our own popular culture, there may be more widespread ignorance about schizophrenia than any other common illness. Ask a classroom of

American college students – in engineering or English literature – what they know about AIDS or cancer and they will probably have a lot to say. But ask about schizophrenia and the silence will be embarrassing. Although schizophrenia is more common than AIDS/HIV, most people know far less about it. "Isn't it like multiple personality disorder?" people ask. "Is it caused by child abuse?" "Are they mentally retarded?" The answer to all these questions is "No."

What is it about this condition that stifles discussion and learning? AIDS, cancer and schizophrenia are all perceived as contaminating and incurable, but somehow people with schizophrenia are seen as more mysterious, alien and violent. Centuries of fear have promulgated many myths about schizophrenia. What are the facts?

Schizophrenia is a psychosis. That is to say, it is a severe mental disorder in which the person's emotions, thinking, judgment, and grasp of reality are so disturbed that his or her functioning is seriously impaired.

The symptoms of schizophrenia are often divided into "positive" and "negative." Positive symptoms are abnormal experiences and perceptions like delusions, hallucinations, illogical and disorganized thinking and inappropriate behavior. Negative symptoms are the absence of normal thoughts, emotions and behavior such as blunted emotions, loss of drive, poverty of thought, and social withdrawal.

Diagnostic difficulties

Problems abound in defining schizophrenia. The two most common functional psychoses are schizophrenia and bipolar disorder (also known as manic-depressive illness). The distinction between the two is not easy to make and psychiatrists in different parts of the world at different times have drawn the boundaries in different ways. Bipolar disorder is an episodic disorder in which psychotic symptoms are associated with severe alterations in mood – at times elated, agitated episodes of mania, at other times depression, with physical and mental slowing, despair, guilt and low self-esteem.

On the other hand, the course of schizophrenia, though fluctuating, tends to be more continuous, and the person's display of emotion is likely to be incongruous or lacking in spontaneity. Markedly illogical thinking is common in schizophrenia. Auditory hallucinations may occur in either manic-depressive illness or schizophrenia, but in schizophrenia they are more likely to be commenting on the person's actions or to be conversing one with another. Delusions, also, can occur in both conditions; in schizo-phrenia they may give the individual the sense that he or she is being controlled by outside forces or that his or her thoughts are being broadcast or interfered with.

Despite common features, different forms of schizophrenia are quite dissimilar. One person, for example, may be paranoid but show good judgment and high functioning in many areas of life. Another may be bizarre in manner and appearance, preoccupied with delusions of bodily disorder, passive and withdrawn. So marked are the differences, in fact, that many experts believe that, when the causes of schizophrenia are worked out, the illness will prove to be a set of different conditions which lead, via a final common pathway of biochemical interactions, to similar consequences.

It is not at all clear what is schizophrenia and what is not. Scandinavian psychiatrists have tended to use a narrow definition of the illness with an emphasis on poor outcome. Russian psychiatrists have adhered to a broad definition with an emphasis on social adjustment. In the United States the diagnostic approach to schizophrenia used to be very broad. With the publication, in 1980, of the third edition of the American Psychiatric Association's *Diagnostic and Statistical Manual*, however, American psychiatry switched from one of the broadest concepts of schizophrenia in the world to one of the narrowest.

Why is the diagnosis so susceptible to fashion? The underlying problem is that schizophrenia and manic-depressive illness share many common symptoms. During an acute episode it is often not possible to tell them apart without knowing the prior history of the illness. The records of people with manic-depressive illness, however, should reveal prior episodes of depression and mania with interludes of normal functioning.

Schizophrenia is universal

We should not let confusion about differentiating schizophrenia from other psychoses detract from the fact that schizophrenia is a universal condition and an ancient one. Typical cases may be distinguished in the medical writings of ancient Greece and Rome, and the condition occurs today in every human society. While the content of delusions and hallucinations varies from culture to culture, the form of the illness is similar everywhere. Two World Health Organization studies, applying a standardized diagnostic approach, have identified characteristic cases of schizophrenia in developed and developing countries from many parts of the globe (World Health Organization, 1979; Jablensky *et al.*, 1992).

More surprisingly, one of these studies (Jablensky *et al.*, 1992) demonstrated that the rate of occurrence of new cases (the incidence) of the condition is similar in every country studied, from India to Ireland. However, since both death and recovery rates for people with psychosis are higher in the developing world, the point prevalence of schizophrenia (the number of cases to be found at any time) is lower in the developing world – around 3 per 1,000 of the population compared to 6 per 1,000 in the developed world (Warner and de Girolamo, 1995). The risk of developing the illness at some time in one's life (the lifetime prevalence) is a little higher – around 1 per cent of the population in the developed world.

People recover from schizophrenia

The popular and professional view that schizophrenia has a progressive, downhill course with universally poor outcome is a myth. Over the course of months or years, about 20 to 25 per cent of people with schizophrenia recover completely from the illness – all their psychotic symptoms disappear and they return to their previous level of functioning. Another 20 per cent continue to have some symptoms, but they are able to lead satisfying and productive lives (Warner, 1994).

In the developing countries, recovery rates are even better. The two World Health Organization studies mentioned above (World Health Organization, 1979; Jablensky *et al.*, 1992) have shown that good outcome occurs in about twice as many patients diagnosed with schizophrenia in the developing world as in the developed world. The reason for the better outcome in the developing world is not completely understood, but it may be that many people with mental illness in developing world villages are better accepted, less stigmatized, and more likely to find work in a subsistence agricultural economy (Warner, 1994).

The course of schizophrenia

Wide variation occurs in the course of schizophrenia. In some cases the onset of illness is gradual, extending over the course of months or years; in others it can begin suddenly, within hours or days. Some people have episodes of illness lasting weeks or months with full remission of symptoms between each episode; others have a fluctuating course in which symptoms are continuous; others again have very little variation in their symptoms of illness over the course of years. The final outcome from the illness in late life can be complete recovery, a mild level of disturbance or continued severe illness.

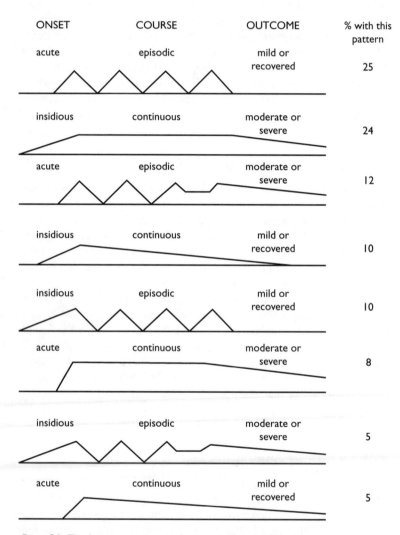

Figure 1.2 The long-term course of schizophrenia in 228 patients
Source: Ciompi (1980)

Figure I.2 is an illustration of the onset, course and outcome of the illness in 228 people with schizophrenia followed into old age by the Swiss psychiatrist, Luc Ciompi (1980). He found that the onset of the illness was either acute (with less than six months from first symptoms to full-blown psychosis) or, conversely, insidious, in roughly equal numbers of cases. Similarly, the course of the condition was episodic or continuous in approximately equal numbers of patients; and the outcome was moderate to severe disability in half the cases and mild disability or full recovery in the other half. Full recovery was observed in more than a quarter of the patients. It is clear that the course of schizophrenia varies a good deal between individuals and that the outcome is often favorable.

It is also true to say that schizophrenia usually becomes less severe as the person with the illness grows older. In addition, the later the illness begins in life, the milder it proves to be. Women usually develop their first symptoms of schizophrenia later than men and the course of their illness tends to be less severe. Onset of schizophrenia before the age of 14 is rare, but when it does begin this early it is associated with a severe course of illness. Onset after the age of 40 is also rare, and is associated with a milder course.

What causes schizophrenia?

There is no single organic defect or infectious agent which causes schizophrenia, but a variety of factors increase the risk of getting the illness – among them, genetics and obstetric complications.

Genetics

Relatives of people with schizophrenia have a greater risk of developing the illness, the risk being progressively higher among those who are more genetically similar to the person with schizophrenia (see Figure I.3). For a nephew or aunt the lifetime risk is about 2 per cent (twice the risk for someone in the general population); for a sibling, parent or child the risk is about 10 per cent (6 to 13 per cent), and for an identical twin (genetically identical to the person with schizophrenia) the risk is close to 50 per cent (Gottesman, 1991).

Studies of people adopted in infancy reveal that the increased risk of schizophrenia among the relatives of people with the illness is due to inheritance rather than environment. The children of people with schizophrenia have the same increased prevalence of the illness whether

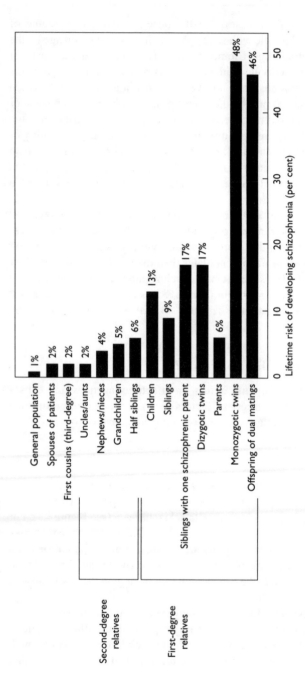

Figure 1.3 The average risk of developing schizophrenia for relatives of a person with the illness; compiled from family and twin studies conducted in Europe between 1920 and 1987

Source: Reprinted by permission of the author. From Gottesman (1991, p. 96). © 1991 Irving I. Gottesman

they are raised by their biological parent with schizophrenia or by adoptive parents (Gottesman, 1991; Warner and de Girolamo, 1995).

There is evidence implicating several genes in causing schizophrenia (Wang *et al.*, 1995; Freedman *et al.*, 1997), and it is likely that more than one is responsible, either through an interactive effect or by producing different variants of the disorder.

Obstetric complications

Since the identical twin of a person with schizophrenia only has a 50 per cent risk of developing the illness, we know that genetics alone do not explain why someone gets the illness. Other powerful factors have to play a part; one of these factors is problems of pregnancy and delivery. The risk for people born with obstetric complications, such as prolonged labor, is double the risk for those born with none. A history of obstetric complications has been found in up to 40 per cent of patients with schizophrenia, making it a major risk factor. This issue will be discussed in detail in Chapter 1.

Viruses

The risk of intrauterine brain damage is increased if a pregnant woman contracts a viral illness. We know that more people with schizophrenia are born in the late winter or spring than at other times of the year, and that this birth bulge sometimes increases after epidemics of viral illnesses like influenza, measles and chickenpox. Maternal viral infections, however, probably account for only a small part of the increased risk for schizophrenia (Warner and de Girolamo, 1995).

Poor parenting does not cause schizophrenia

Contrary to the beliefs of professionals prior to the 1970s and to the impression still promoted by the popular media, there is no evidence, even after decades of research, that family or parenting problems cause schizophrenia.

As early as 1948, psychoanalysts proposed that mothers fostered schizophrenia in their offspring through cold and distant parenting (Fromm-Reichmann, 1948). Others blamed parental schisms, and confusing patterns of communication within the family (Lidz *et al.*, 1965; Laing and Esterton, 1970). The double-bind theory, put forward by anthropologist Gregory Bateson, argued that schizophrenia is promoted by contradictory parental messages from which the child is unable to escape (Bateson *et al.*, 1956). While enjoying broad public recognition, such theories have seldom been adequately tested, and none of the research satisfactorily resolves the question of whether differences found in the families of people with schizophrenia are the *cause* or the *effect* of psychological abnormalities in the disturbed family member (Hirsch and Leff, 1975).

Millions of relatives of people with schizophrenia have suffered needless shame, guilt and stigma because of this widespread misconception.

Drug abuse does not cause schizophrenia

Hallucinogenic drugs like LSD can induce short-lasting episodes of psychosis, and the heavy use of marijuana and stimulant drugs like cocaine and amphetamines may precipitate brief, toxic psychoses with features similar to schizophrenia (Bowers, 1987; Tennent and Groesbeck, 1972). It is also possible, though by no means certain, that drug abuse can trigger the onset of schizophrenia.

Relatives of a person with schizophrenia sometimes blame hallucinogenic drugs for causing the illness, but they are mistaken. We know this because, in the 1950s and 1960s, LSD was used as an experimental drug in psychiatry in Britain and America. The proportion of the volunteers and patients who developed a long-lasting psychosis like schizophrenia was scarcely greater than in the general population (S. Cohen, 1960; Malleson, 1971). It is true that a Swedish study found that army conscripts who used marijuana heavily were six times more likely to develop schizophrenia later in life (Andreasson *et al.*, 1987), but this was probably because those people who were destined to develop schizophrenia were more likely to use marijuana as a way to cope with the pre-morbid symptoms of the illness.

This question will be discussed in more detail in Chapter 2.

The brain in schizophrenia

Physical changes in the brain have been identified in some people with schizophrenia. The analysis of brain tissue after death has revealed a number of structural abnormalities, and new brain-imaging techniques have revealed changes in both the structure and function of the brain during life. Techniques such as magnetic resonance imaging (MRI) reveal changes in the size of different parts of the brain, especially in the temporal lobes. The fluid-filled spaces (the ventricles) in the interior of the temporal lobes are often enlarged and the temporal lobe tissue diminished. The greater the observed changes the greater the severity of the person's thought disorder and his or her auditory hallucinations (Suddath *et al.*, 1990).

Some imaging techniques, such as positron emission tomography (PET), measure the actual functioning of the brain and provide a similar picture of abnormality. PET scanning reveals hyperactivity in the temporal lobes, particularly in the hippocampus, a part of the temporal lobe concerned with orientation and very short-term memory (Tamminga *et al.*, 1992). Another type of functional imaging, electrophysiological brain recording using EEG tracings, shows that most people with schizophrenia seem to be excessively responsive to repeated environmental stimuli and more limited in their ability to blot out irrelevant information (Freedman *et al.*, 1997). In line with this finding, those parts of the brain that are supposed to screen out irrelevant stimuli, such as the frontal lobe, show decreased activity on PET scan (Tamminga *et al.*, 1992).

Tying in with this sensory screening difficulty, post-mortem brain tissue examination has revealed problems in a certain type of brain cell – the inhibitory interneuron. These neurons damp down the action of the principal nerve cells, preventing them from responding to too many inputs. Thus, they prevent the brain from being overwhelmed by too much sensory information from the environment. The chemical messengers or neurotransmitters (primarily gamma-amino butyric acid or GABA) released by these interneurons are diminished in the brains of people with schizophrenia (Benes *et al.*, 1991; Akbarian *et al.*, 1993), suggesting that there is less inhibition of brain overload.

Abnormality in the functioning of these interneurons appears to produce changes in the brain cells that release the neurotransmitter dopamine. The role of dopamine has long been of interest to schizophrenia researchers, because drugs such as amphetamines that increase dopamine's effects can cause psychoses that resemble schizophrenia, and drugs that block or decrease dopamine's effect are useful for the treatment of psychoses (Meltzer and Stahl, 1976). Dopamine increases the sensitivity of brain cells to stimuli. Ordinarily, this heightened awareness is useful in increasing a person's awareness during times of stress or danger, but, for a person with schizophrenia, the addition of the effect of dopamine to an already hyperactive brain state may tip the person into psychosis.

These findings suggest that in schizophrenia there is a deficit in the regulation of brain activity by interneurons, so that the brain over-responds to the many signals in the environment and lacks the ability to screen out unwanted stimuli. This problem is made worse by a decrease in the size of the temporal lobes, which ordinarily process sensory inputs, making it more difficult for the person to respond appropriately to new stimuli.

Why does schizophrenia begin after puberty?

Schizophrenia researchers have long been puzzled about why the illness normally begins in adolescence when important risk factors, such as genetic loading and neonatal brain damage, are present from birth or sooner. Many believe that the answer to this puzzle could tell us a lot about the cause of the illness. We now have some good clues to this mystery.

We know, for example, that normal brain development leads to the loss of 30 to 40 per cent of the connections (synapses) between brain cells during the developmental period from early life to adolescence (Huttenlocher, 1979). Brain cells themselves do not diminish in number during this period, only their connectivity. It appears that we may need a high degree of connectivity between brain cells in infancy to enhance our ability to learn language rapidly (toddlers learn as many as twelve new words a day). The loss of neurons during later childhood and adolescence, however, improves our "working memory" and our efficiency in processing complex linguistic information (Hoffman and McGlashan, 1997). When we are listening to someone talking, for example, and we miss part of a phrase or sentence because someone nearby coughs or sneezes, our working memory allows us to fill in the blank, using a memory store of similar familiar phrases we have heard before.

We now know that, for people with schizophrenia, this normally useful process of synaptic pruning has been carried too far, leaving fewer synapses in the frontal lobes and medial temporal cortex (Feinberg, 1983). In consequence, there are deficits in the interaction between these two areas of the brain in schizophrenia, which reduce the adequacy of working memory (Weinberger et al., 1992). One intriguing computer modeling exercise suggests that decreasing synaptic connections and eroding working memory in this way leads not only to abnormalities in the ability to recognize meaning when stimuli are ambiguous but also to the development of auditory hallucinations (Hoffman and McGlashan, 1997).

It is possible, therefore, that this natural and adaptive process of synaptic elimination in childhood, if carried too far, could lead to the development of schizophrenia (Feinberg, 1983). If true, this would help explain why schizophrenia persists among humans despite its obvious functional disadvantages and its association with reduced fertility. The genes for synaptic pruning may help us refine our capacity to comprehend speech and other complex stimuli, but, when complicated by environmental assaults resulting in brain injury, the result could be symptoms of psychosis. As yet, this formulation is speculative, but it allows us to see more clearly how the environment may interact with our innate qualities to increase our predisposition to schizophrenia.

What works?

There is more agreement now about what is important in the treatment of schizophrenia than ever before. In a recent global project designed to combat the stigma of schizophrenia (see Chapter 10), prominent psychiatrists from around the world agreed on the following principles:

- People with schizophrenia can be treated effectively in a variety of settings. These days the use of hospitals is mainly reserved for those in an acute relapse. Outside of the hospital, a range of alternative treatment settings have been devised which provide supervision and support and are less alienating and coercive than the hospital.
- Family involvement can improve the effectiveness of treatment. A solid body of research has demonstrated that relapse in schizophrenia is much less frequent when families are provided with support and education about schizophrenia.
- Medications are an important part of treatment but they are only part of the answer. They can reduce or eliminate positive symptoms but they have a negligible effect on negative symptoms. Fortunately, modern, novel antipsychotic medications, introduced in the past few years, can provide benefits while causing less severe side effects than the standard antipsychotic drugs that were introduced in the mid-1950s.
- Treatment should include social rehabilitation. People with schizophrenia usually need help to improve their functioning in the community. This can include training in basic living skills; assistance with a host of day-to-day tasks; and job training, job placement, and work support.
- Work helps people recover from schizophrenia. Productive activity is basic to a person's sense of identity and worth. The availability of work in a subsistence economy may be one of the main reasons that

outcome from schizophrenia is so much better in villages in the developing world. Given training and support, most people with schizophrenia can work.

- People with schizophrenia can get worse if treated punitively or confined unnecessarily. Extended hospital stays are rarely necessary if good community treatment is available. Jail and prison are not appropriate places of care. Yet, around the world, large numbers of people with schizophrenia are housed in prison cells, usually charged with minor crimes, largely because of the lack of adequate community treatment.
- People with schizophrenia and their family members should help plan and even deliver treatment. Consumers of mental health services can be successfully employed in treatment programs, and when they help train treatment staff, professional attitudes and patient outcome both improve.
- People's responses towards someone with schizophrenia influence the person's course of illness and quality of life. Negative attitudes can push people with schizophrenia and their families into hiding the illness and drive them away from help. If people with schizophrenia are shunned and feared they cannot be genuine members of their own community. They become isolated and victims of discrimination in employment, accommodation and education.

This is where we are now. This book will take off from these accepted facts and practices and make suggestions about how we can go forward to a level of knowledge and a set of treatment approaches, social policies and community responses that will limit the occurrence of new cases and allow people with schizophrenia and their families to lead fuller and more satisfying lives.

Part I

Individual level

Chapter 1

Obstetric complications

A genetic predisposition to schizophrenia may be present in as many as 7 to 10 per cent of the population. This is the assumption made by genetic researchers doing linkage studies (Wang *et al.*, 1995; Freedman *et al.*, 1997). Yet, as mentioned in the Introduction, the illness becomes manifest in no more than 1 per cent of the population (Warner and de Girolamo, 1995). Since only a fraction of those genetically at risk develop the illness, we have to assume that either it takes more than one gene to cause the illness or that the addition of an environmental factor is necessary. We know, in fact, that non-genetic, environmental factors are essential, because, despite being genetically indistinguishable, the identical twin of someone with schizophrenia has only a 50 per cent chance of developing the illness, not a 100 per cent chance (see Figure I.3). Preeminent among these causative environmental factors, it emerges, are complications of pregnancy and delivery.

A review and meta-analysis of all the studies conducted prior to mid-1994 on the influence of obstetric complications, reveals that complications before and around the time of birth appear to double the risk of developing schizophrenia (though this apparent effect could be inflated by the tendency for journals to publish studies with positive results) (Geddes and Lawrie, 1995). Since this analysis was published, more recent studies have shown similar results. Studies using data gathered at the time of birth from very large cohorts of children born in Finland and Sweden in the 1960s and 1970s reveal that various obstetric complications double or triple the risk of developing schizophrenia (Hultman *et al.*, 1999; Dalman *et al.*, 1999; P. B. Jones *et al.*, 1998). A recent American study shows that the risk of schizophrenia is more than four times greater in those who experience oxygen deprivation before or at the time of birth, and that such complications increase the risk of schizophrenia much more than other psychoses like bipolar disorder (Zornberg *et al.*, 2000).

Obstetric complications are a statistically important risk factor because they are so common. In the general population, they occur in up to 40 per cent of births (the precise rate of occurrence depending on how they are defined) (McNeil, 1988; Geddes and Lawrie, 1995; Sacker *et al.*, 1996). They are, therefore, a much more prominent cause of schizophrenia than maternal viral infection, which probably explains no more than 2 per cent of cases of the illness (Sham *et al.*, 1992). The authors of the meta-analysis estimate that complications of pregnancy and delivery increase the prevalence of schizophrenia by 20 per cent (Geddes and Lawrie, 1995).

The obstetric complications most closely associated with the increased risk of developing schizophrenia are those which induce fetal oxygen deprivation, particularly prolonged labor (McNeil, 1988), and placental complications (P. B. Jones *et al.*, 1998; Hultman *et al.*, 1999; Dalman *et al.*, 1999). Early delivery, often provoked by complications of pregnancy, is also more common for those who go on to develop schizophrenia, and infants who suffer perinatal brain damage are at a much increased risk of subsequent schizophrenia (P. B. Jones *et al.*, 1998). Trauma at the time of labor and delivery, and especially prolonged labor, is associated with an increase in structural brain abnormalities – cerebral atrophy and small hippocampi – which occur frequently in schizophrenia (McNeil *et al.*, 2000).

Ironically, these complications are particularly common among infants who already have a high risk for developing schizophrenia – the children of people who themselves suffer from the illness. For people with schizophrenia, the risk that any one of their children will develop schizophrenia approaches 10 per cent, and, where both parents suffer from the illness, the risk for each child is close to 50 per cent (Gottesman, 1991). (See Figure I.3.) But this hazard is compounded by the fact that women with schizophrenia are more likely than other women to experience complications of pregnancy. For women with schizophrenia, the risk of premature delivery and of bearing low birth-weight children is increased by as much as 50 per cent (Bennedsen, 1999; Sacker *et al.*, 1996). This is to a great extent a result of the fact that women with schizophrenia (and other psychiatric illnesses) receive less adequate prenatal care than others in the general population (Kelly *et al.*, 1999).

The increased risk of complications for pregnant women with schizophrenia could also be due to their higher rates of smoking, to their use of alcohol and other substances, or to poverty. It might, theoretically, also be caused by a gene which increases the risk of both schizophrenia and obstetric complications, but this does not appear to be the case. One group of researchers point out that the increased risk of obstetric complications occurs when the mother, but not the father, suffers from schizophrenia; a genetically determined risk of obstetric complications and schizophrenia would not be confined just to the mother (Sacker *et al.*, 1996).

Another group points out that a genetic link between obstetric complications and schizophrenia is unlikely because there is no increase in risk of obstetric complications in those who have a family history of schizophrenia (and, therefore, a greater likelihood of carrying a gene for the illness) (Marcelis *et al.*, 1998). Whatever the cause, the result of the obstetric complications is to further increase the risk of schizophrenia in the offspring of women with schizophrenia.

On a positive note, there is good evidence that improved obstetric care can lead to a lower incidence of schizophrenia. The large majority of recent epidemiological studies looking at changes in the incidence of schizophrenia in countries around the world indicate a substantial decrease in the occurrence of the illness since the Second World War. Several studies from Britain, Scandinavia and New Zealand reveal a decrease in the incidence of schizophrenia of the order of 40 to 60 per cent over 10- to 15-year time-spans during the period from the late 1960s to the late 1980s (Warner and de Girolamo, 1995). It is unclear, however, to what extent the apparent decline is an artifact resulting from changes in diagnosis and treatment patterns.

It is possible, for example, that, as diagnostic practices change, fewer patients with a psychotic illness are being labeled as suffering from schizophrenia and more are being labeled as having bipolar disorder. Similarly, fewer cases of schizophrenia may have been detected in recent years because more are being treated in the community and are never admitted to hospital. While it is likely that such artifacts as these explain some of the apparent decrease in the incidence of schizophrenia, it is not at all clear that they explain all of it, and a real drop in the occurrence of the illness appears possible (Warner and de Girolamo, 1995).

Many researchers argue that, if real, the explanation for the declining occurrence of schizophrenia in the developed world is the improvement in obstetric care in the postwar period. The decline in the occurrence of schizophrenia in England and Wales parallels a decrease in the infant mortality rate, with a twenty-year delay – just what one would expect for an illness which begins, on average, around age 20, if improvements in obstetric care were responsible for the change (Gupta and Murray, 1991). If the quality of obstetric care and a reduction in complications are important in bringing about changes in the incidence of schizophrenia, this would help to explain why the decrease has been greatest in the most prosperous regions of Britain (Gupta and Murray, 1991), and why the districts showing no decrease are those with high rates of poverty and large immigrant populations (Eagles, 1991). Obstetric complications are more common among the poor and immigrants; children born to Afro-Caribbean immigrants, for example, are more likely to be of low birth weight than those in the general population (Terry *et al.*, 1987; Griffiths *et al.*, 1989).

It seems probable, therefore, that minimizing obstetric complications will lead to further reductions in the occurrence of schizophrenia, particularly if we target those who are at greatest risk for bearing children who will develop the illness.

Intervention no. I

An educational campaign on the risks of obstetric complications

We could decrease the incidence of schizophrenia by educating people with schizophrenia and their relatives (particularly those of or approaching child-bearing years) about the added risk of schizophrenia from complications of pregnancy and delivery which contribute to perinatal brain injury. Prospective mothers should be cautioned that smoking in pregnancy or maternal illnesses such as diabetes and heart disease may contribute to chronic fetal hypoxia and increase the risk of schizophrenia in the offspring. Where one or both parents has a family history of schizophrenia, obstetricians should be aware that fetal oxygen deprivation, prolonged labor, placental complications and conditions of pregnancy leading to early delivery and low birth weight may present an added risk of schizophrenia to the newborn later in life. In such cases it would be appropriate to establish a low risk-threshold for the use of caesarian section and to take aggressive precautions to prevent early delivery and low birth weight.

One of the most effective interventions would be to ensure that all women with schizophrenia get adequate prenatal care, which is the opposite of what currently happens (Kelly *et al.*, 1999). Several studies have shown that the provision of adequate prenatal care leads to better obstetric outcomes and fewer low birth-weight babies. For example, the babies of cocaine-using women in New York who attended four or more prenatal appointments were half a pound (a quarter of a kilogram) heavier, on average, than those whose mothers attended three appointments or fewer (Racine *et al.*, 1993). Similarly, the birth weight of babies of cocaine users who were enrolled in a comprehensive program of prenatal care in Chicago was more than a pound and a half (three-quarters of a kilogram) greater than for women who had made two or fewer prenatal visits (MacGregor *et al.*, 1989). The same benefits of prenatal care accrue to the infants of mothers who are not cocaine users (Zuckerman *et al.*, 1989).

To avoid creating undue concern, the educational efforts suggested here should make it clear that the risk to a person who is a first-degree relative of someone with schizophrenia, of bearing a child who will develop the illness, is not frighteningly high. As indicated in the Introduction (see Figure I.3), the risk is increased from the general population rate of 1 per cent to around 2 to 5 per cent, (because the infant will be a second-degree relative of the person with schizophrenia) but the risk may be reduced by averting complications of pregnancy and delivery.

To provide the necessary education, we could:

- establish an international panel of psychiatric epidemiologists and obstetricians to review the current data on obstetric complications and the risk of schizophrenia and write a report that includes recommendations for obstetric counseling and practice;
- publish the panel report in major obstetric and psychiatric journals;
- produce and distribute informational brochures summarizing the recommendations so that they can be placed in waiting rooms of mental health agencies throughout the developed world;
- train junior doctors in primary care, psychiatry and obstetrics to provide genetic and obstetric counseling to people with schizophrenia and their families.

With such an intervention, we could decrease the number of people who suffer from this dreadful illness, the associated suffering of family members and the enormous costs to society.

Chapter 2

Substance use

Mental health professionals in the United States have generally been more concerned about the use of street drugs and alcohol by people with schizophrenia and other serious mental illnesses than have professionals in Europe. In the US, the issue has been termed a "crisis" (V. B. Brown *et al.*, 1989), and American psychiatric journals often carry articles on the topic. Is this an American over-reaction, or is the concern justified?

Frequency of use

In fact, the frequency with which people with schizophrenia use drugs of abuse is greater in the US. A recent study shows that people with serious mental illness in Bologna, Italy, are substantially less likely than those in Boulder, Colorado, to have used a variety of substances (Fioritti *et al.*, 1997). Only a quarter of the people with mental illness from Bologna used marijuana at some time in their lives compared to nearly 90 per cent of subjects in Boulder. The use of hallucinogens, stimulants, narcotics and solvents by people with mental illness is also higher in Boulder (see Table 2.1).

In general, these differences for people with mental illness match differences in the market availability of illicit drugs in the two countries. The only substances more commonly abused by people with mental illness in Bologna are over-the-counter preparations. However, even the abuse of alcohol and the inhaling of solvents, glue, paint and gasoline, although these substances are all equally available in Italy, are more frequent among people with mental illness in Boulder than in Bologna. It is likely that the greater use among the American patients matches patterns of use in the general US population. Over 30 per cent of American adults between the ages of 19 and 30, for example, use marijuana, and nearly half that number are using cocaine (Johnston *et al.*, 1989). In addition,

Table 2.1 Lifetime frequency of substance use by people with serious mental illness in Bologna, Italy and Boulder, Colorado (per cent)

	Bologna	Boulder
Alcohol (to intoxication)	56	93
Marijuana	25	89
Hallucinogens	11	62
Stimulants (except cocaine)	25	51
Cocaine	14	49
Narcotics	25	46
Solvents	14	29
Over-the-counter remedies	28	13

the life circumstances of people with mental illness in Boulder, which, as we shall see in Chapter 5, are distinctly different from those in Bologna, may contribute to their elevated use of substances. For example, the heavy use of marijuana by people with mental illness in Boulder was associated with being unemployed and lacking other daily activity (Warner *et al.*, 1994), and in both countries substance use was often reported to be an attempt to reduce boredom.

Do people with schizophrenia use more substances?

It seems to be true that people with schizophrenia use more drugs than others in the population. In one large study of mental disorder carried out in several American cities, the Epidemiologic Catchment Area (ECA) study, the prevalence of substance abuse at some time in the person's life was as high as 47 per cent of people with schizophrenia, compared to 17 per cent of people in the general population (Regier *et al.*, 1990). Similarly *current* substance abuse rates in different samples of Americans with schizophrenia, running at 30 to 40 per cent (Atkinson, 1973; Safer, 1985), are substantially higher than the ECA rate of 15 per cent (Regier *et al.*, 1990).

There is less agreement, however, about which drugs tend to be used more by people with schizophrenia. Two different reviews of the literature conclude that people with schizophrenia tend to use hallucinogens and stimulants (like amphetamines and cocaine) more than do people in the general population, but they disagree about whether marijuana use is greater. Both reviews conclude that the use of alcohol, sedatives and narcotics is no greater among people with schizophrenia (Mueser *et al.*, 1990; Schneier and Siris, 1987).

It is clear that people with schizophrenia smoke more tobacco than others. In an Irish study, for example, more than 80 per cent of subjects with schizophrenia smoked cigarettes, compared to less than 40 per cent of the general population, and those who smoked were likely to be heavy users and to smoke high-tar brands (Masterson and O'Shea, 1984). In a recent Scottish study, nearly 60 per cent of people with schizophrenia were smokers, compared to under 30 per cent of the general population, and those who smoked were heavy smokers (McCreadie and Kelly, 2000). The authors of the Scottish study concluded that people with schizophrenia were spending around a quarter of their income on cigarettes and, given the high sales tax on tobacco in Britain, that the tax revenue from their smoking covered anywhere from a fifth to a third of the direct costs of treating schizophrenia in Britain. Needless to say, this heavy smoking increases health hazards such as emphysema, though, curiously, the lung cancer risk is not elevated in schizophrenia (Masterson and O'Shea, 1984; Gulbinat et al., 1992). There is an illness-related reason for this heavy use of tobacco. As mentioned in the Introduction, most people with schizophrenia are unusually responsive to environmental stimuli and have a limited ability to block out irrelevant sources of information. This neurophysiological abnormality, it emerges, is mediated by nicotine receptors in the brain; and large doses of nicotine, by blocking these receptors, lead to a brief reduction in auditory hallucinations (Freedman et al., 1997). Unfortunately, the dose of nicotine required to achieve this effect is so high and the effect so brief that non-tobacco nicotine in the form of chewing gum or skin patches is inadequate to achieve a therapeutic effect on the symptoms of schizophrenia (Freedman, 1999).

Effect on illness

How do other substances besides nicotine affect people with schizophrenia? The first point to clear up is that, as pointed out in the Introduction, drugs do not cause schizophrenia. Hallucinogens, like LSD, and the heavy use of marijuana and stimulants, like cocaine, can cause brief psychotic episodes with many of the same symptoms as schizophrenia (Bowers, 1987; Tennent and Groesbeck, 1972), but they don't cause a lifelong illness. When LSD was used experimentally in the 1960s it did not appear to increase the risk of schizophrenia in the users (S. Cohen, 1960; Malleson, 1971).

It often seems to family members and other observers that drug use causes schizophrenia because people who develop the illness have often been using drugs before the onset of their first full-blown psychotic episode. In a study we conducted in Boulder of substance use by people with mental illness, we found that most of the people who suffered from schizophrenia, if they used drugs or alcohol at all, began their use of marijuana or hallucinogens before they developed their first positive psychotic symptoms (such as hallucinations or delusions), although the use of stimulants, in nearly every case, began after the first psychotic episode. For patients with bipolar disorder (manic-depressive illness), however, this was not the case; the time at which substance use or abuse began was unrelated to the time of onset of the illness (Taylor and Warner, 1994). One might wonder if this means that the marijuana and hallucinogen use precipitated the onset of the schizophrenic illness. If that were the case, however, the onset of schizophrenia among those who used drugs would have been earlier, and it was not (Taylor and Warner, 1994).

It seems likely that people with schizophrenia, if they use drugs or alcohol, do so before their first full-blown episode of illness because they feel odd, lonely or unhappy, and they are ready to try anything to feel better. Schizophrenia, as we know, is preceded by a long period of prodromal symptoms, and a carefully conducted German study has demonstrated that the onset of drug and alcohol abuse in people with schizophrenia usually follows the very first negative symptom of schizophrenia (such as social withdrawal) but precedes the first positive symptom (such as hallucinations). The authors conclude that substance use is an avenue to the relief of the earliest symptoms of the illness, but not a cause of the illness (Hambrecht and Hafner, 1995). Thus, the finding that Swedish army conscripts who used marijuana heavily before induction to the military were six times more likely to develop schizophrenia later in life (Andreasson et al., 1987), may merely illustrate the way in which people who are in the prodromal stages of schizophrenia use marijuana as a way of coping with the premorbid symptoms of the illness.

Several studies have shown that people with serious mental illness who abuse substances have a worse course of illness (Carpenter et al., 1985; Craig et al., 1985; Safer, 1985; Drake and Wallach, 1989). Other researchers, however, have found psychopathology to be no worse or, sometimes, lower among people with mental illness who use substances (Warner et al., 1994; Zisook et al., 1992; Buckley et al., 1994; Anderson et al., in press). One reason for this discrepancy may lie in the common finding that substance users are also more likely to be noncompliant with treatment (Drake and Wallach, 1989); it may be that the poor course of illness, when it is observed, is a result of this noncompliance rather than a direct consequence of substance use (Anderson *et al.*, in press). In the study conducted by the author and his colleagues in Boulder (Warner *et al.*, 1994), where noncompliance was reduced by assertive case management, substance use by people with serious mental illness was not associated with noncompliance or poor outcome. In fact, we found that psychopathology and hospital admission rates were *lower* among marijuana users than among those who used no substances at all. Similarly, Kim Mueser and colleagues, in two different studies (K. T. Mueser *et al.*, 1990; K. M. Mueser *et al.*, in press), found, as we did, symptoms of anxiety and tension and rates of admission to hospital to be lower among mentally ill marijuana users.

Researchers (Linszen *et al.*, 1994) and clinicians alike have observed that marijuana can precipitate a worsening of positive symptoms in schizophrenia, so it is surprising to discover that, on average, in some samples, use of marijuana is associated with reduced symptoms and lower rates of hospital admission. A clue to understanding this paradox may be picked up from patients' self-reports of the effect of different drugs on their symptoms of mental illness. In our study conducted in Boulder, people with mental illness reported that alcohol and hallucinogens had scarcely any beneficial effects on psychiatric symptoms, and often made them feel worse. In contrast, people who preferred marijuana reported beneficial effects on depression, anxiety, insomnia and physical discomfort, while recognizing that it did not help, or made worse, paranoia and hallucinations. It is possible, as Mary Ann Test and her associates (Test *et al.*, 1989) suggest, that patients adjust the dose of marijuana to obtain "the most advantageous benefit-to-cost ratio" (p. 471) – that is, they tailor drug use to achieve maximal impact on unpleasant affective symptoms, with minimal increase in positive symptoms. It is also possible that patients who experience the worst adverse effects tend to avoid the drug.

While reducing depression, anxiety and insomnia are among the most common reasons that people with mental illness give for using drugs and alcohol, they are by no means the only ones. Over 70 per cent of people with mental illness in Boulder cited "having something to do with friends" as being important, and nearly 60 per cent mentioned combating boredom and over 40 per cent improving self-esteem as important reasons. Unemployment, social isolation and alienation may therefore be significant factors contributing to the high rates of substance use by people with mental illness.

Intervention no. 2

Individualized substance-use counseling

Rigid "twelve-step" substance-abuse programs do not work well with people with serious mental illness (Noordsy *et al*., 1996; Jerrell and Ridgely, 1995) as their reasons for use of substances are so complex. Many in this population feel a need to find relief from chronic affective symptoms and medication side effects. For these reasons, treatment approaches need to be individualized. For example, if a patient is using substances to counter depression, anxiety or restlessness caused by antipsychotic medications, an adjustment in his or medication may help alleviate the problem. A blanket recommendation by the therapist to avoid all substance use may not only be clinically useless but may also be seen by the client as showing a poor understanding of his or her real life problems.

Therapists should be open to the possibility that a substance used by a client with schizophrenia may, in that person's case and with his or her pattern of use, be useful. Marijuana use, for example, may be helping a client feel calmer and happier and be preventing relapse due to stress, or be reducing unpleasant side effects from medication. In another case, or with another pattern of use, the substance may have deleterious effects. Before giving advice, the therapist needs to know, for each substance used, the reasons for use and (from the client's subjective report and the objective evaluation of others) the effects of that substance on the patient's mental state and behavior. If a patient shifts into a more severe course of illness, the therapist should not only consider the possibility that the patient has increased the use of a drug with harmful effects, but also the possibility that the provoking stress may be withdrawal from the routine use of marijuana or some other calming drug.

It would also be valuable to conduct research on the effect of marijuana on patients with schizophrenia. Since it is difficult to use illegal substances in research, it would be appropriate to conduct further naturalistic studies of the effect of the casual use of this substance in different groups of people with schizophrenia who are compliant with treatment.

These suggestions may seem innocuous; it is difficult, however, to publish views like these in an American psychiatric journal. Why are such opinions heresy in American psychiatry? Perhaps because the profession reflects the dominant governmental and cultural stance on substance abuse in a country which emphasizes punishment over treatment and which imposes heavy penalties for relatively minor infringements of the drug laws. In New York state, for example, the *mandatory* sentence for possessing 4 ounces (113 grams) of a narcotic, or for selling 2 ounces (57 grams), is fifteen years in prison. Over 90 per cent of the massive increase in the incarceration of women in New York state during the past ten years, while America has been escalating the "War on Drugs," is accounted for by women held on drug-related offenses. Nationwide, 2 million drug offenders are behind bars. To tolerate drug use by people with mental illness is as difficult as decriminalizing marijuana use by the general public.

This cultural bias, perhaps, prevents a more vigorous attempt to look for social causes of, and solutions to, substance use by people with mental illness. We should try to overcome this bias, however, and examine, in each case, to what extent alienation, unemployment and boredom, for example, are factors increasing the use of drugs and alcohol by people with mental illness. If we are to decrease the harmful and expensive consequences of substance use by people with schizophrenia – deterioration of health, failure to care for one's basic needs and hospital admission – we may need to invest more in those programs that can help a person find a place in the world, that help people make friends and fulfill useful social roles – such programs as supported employment, psychosocial clubhouses, and consumer-run businesses (all of which will be discussed further in Chapter 8).

Chapter 3

Social stress

The research reveals that stress can trigger episodes of schizophrenia. People with schizophrenia are more likely to report a stressful life event preceding an episode of illness than during a period of remission. Similarly, stressful events are more likely to occur prior to an episode of schizophrenia than in the same time period for people drawn from the general population (Rabkin, 1982). For example, in a study from London, 46 per cent of a group of people with schizophrenia experienced a life event that was independent of their own actions in the three weeks before an episode of illness (including, in some cases, the first episode of illness), compared to only 12 per cent of healthy population controls (Brown and Birley, 1968). It appears that stress can precipitate episodes of illness in people who suffer from schizophrenia and that, although stress does not cause the illness, it can influence the timing of the first episode of schizophrenia.

The research also indicates that the life events occurring before episodes of schizophrenia are milder and less objectively troublesome than those before episodes of other disorders such as depression (Beck and Worthen, 1972). This sensitivity to mild stress may explain why some studies do not show big differences in the response of people with schizophrenia to stress; the cut-off level of stress in the research may be set too high to show an effect. Ironically, given the exquisite sensitivity of people with schizophrenia to stress, the research shows that the chronic stress level is inflated above normal for many people who suffer from this illness (Rabkin, 1982), adding to their vulnerability to relapse.

These findings make sense when we recall (see the Introduction) that in schizophrenia there is a deficit in the regulation of brain activity so that the brain over-responds to environmental stimuli, reducing the person's ability to regulate his or her response to new stresses.

Stress and drug treatment

Antipsychotic drugs appear to be more important in preventing relapse in schizophrenia for people living under stressful conditions, and of less importance for those in settings where stress is milder. As British social psychiatrist John Wing put it:

> Drug treatment and social treatments are not alternatives but must be used to complement each other. The better the environmental conditions, the less the need for medication: the poorer the social milieu, the greater the need (or at least the use) of drugs.
>
> (Wing, 1978, p. 1335)

Several pieces of research support this view. A series of studies, discussed in detail in Chapter 6, has shown that the relapse rate is higher for people with schizophrenia who live with critical or over-involved relatives than for those whose relatives are more supportive and less smothering. In the earliest of these studies, conducted in London, it was found that the relapse rate for patients living in more stressful households could be reduced either by limiting contact between the patient and his or her relatives or by using antipsychotic medication. For patients living in low-stress families, however, the relapse rate was low regardless of whether they were taking medicine or not (Brown *et al.*, 1972; Vaughn and Leff, 1976). With longer follow-up, it emerged that antipsychotic medication was of some benefit to the patients in low-stress homes. Relapse in patients in low-stress homes was only likely to occur if they were subjected to additional independent stressful events, such as job loss, and medication appeared to be of value in protecting patients against the effect of such acute stresses (Leff and Vaughn, 1980, 1981).

The stress-reducing effect of a supportive human environment has been demonstrated in other British studies. Heart-rate and skin-conductance tests have shown that people with schizophrenia have a higher level of arousal than normal individuals, irrespective of whether they are living in high- or low-stress households. This heightened level of arousal drops to normal when the person with schizophrenia is in the company of a non-stressful relative but continues at an elevated rate when he or she is in the company of a critical or over-involved relative. The finding holds true for people with schizophrenia in an acute psychotic episode (Sturgeon *et al.*, 1981) and for those in remission (Tarrier *et al.*, 1979).

Successful and unsuccessful interventions

The level of arousal in people with schizophrenia in residential treatment can be controlled by creating an environment that is optimally stimulating and supportive. In such settings drug dosage need not be as high. Drug doses for people with schizophrenia were consistently lower in such progressive psychosocial treatment programs as Gordon Paul's unit at Illinois State Hospital (Paul *et al.*, 1972), William Carpenter's program at the National Institute of Mental Health (NIMH) (Carpenter *et al.*, 1977), Loren Mosher's two Soteria House projects in California (Mosher, 1995), and Luc Ciompi's Soteria Berne in Switzerland (Ciompi *et al.*, 1995). All of these programs developed individualized treatment interventions in low-stress environments in which the alienating aspects of the institution were reduced to a minimum.

As we will see in Chapter 6, interventions aimed at minimizing the impact of domestic stress on people with schizophrenia through family psychoeducational approaches have also proven successful in reducing the relapse rate (Leff and Vaughn, 1985; Falloon *et al.*, 1984).

Overly stimulating treatment, on the other hand, can increase stress, arousal and relapse in schizophrenia. In a study conducted by Solomon Goldberg and associates at NIMH, outpatients suffering from schizo-phrenia were randomly allocated to either routine outpatient care or a more intensive program of "major role therapy," a combination of social casework and vocational counseling. The more severely ill patients relapsed *sooner* if they were receiving the intensive social therapy. The main thrust of the therapy was to urge "the patient to become more responsible and to expand his horizons" (Goldberg *et al.*, 1977, p. 171). The authors concluded that the therapy was too intrusive and stressful and had a toxic effect similar to that of critical and over-involved relatives.

We may conclude that when people with schizophrenia are in an environment which is protective but not regressive, stimulating but not stressful, and warm but not intrusive (whether it be a family home, their own apartment or a residential treatment setting), many will need less antipsychotic medication. On the other hand, people with schizophrenia who are exposed to significant stress (whether it be intrusive relatives, over-enthusiastic psychotherapy or homelessness, hunger, or poverty) will have a higher relapse rate and will have to rely on higher doses of medication to achieve adequate functioning.

Housing, income and employment

In recent decades, since the advent of deinstitutionalization, too few people with schizophrenia have been placed in suitable therapeutic settings. A third of all the people with schizophrenia in the United States subsist in settings which scarcely pretend to be therapeutic – in jail, on Skid Row, in nursing homes or boarding homes (Warner, 1994).

The research shows us that we should create settings which reduce rather than inflate chronic stress levels. In some cases, this may mean finding accommodation where people with schizophrenia are in the company of relatively stable people rather than with disturbed and disturbing others. In other cases, support and security may be best provided by residential settings which preserve the sense of community generated among the subculture of people with mental illness (Mandiberg, 1999). We should try to establish settings which are secure and life-long, rather than relying on rooms and apartments from which the person with schizophrenia is likely to be evicted whenever he or she suffers a relapse. An example would be using foster families, as in intervention 7 (in Chapter 5). We should create long-term employment opportunities, as in interventions 9, 10 and 11 (Chapters 7 and 8), rather than leaving our clients to wander the streets aimlessly. People with schizophrenia would fare better if they had an adequate income instead of daily being forced to struggle against the consequences of poverty (see interventions 10 and 11 in Chapter 8). As a society, we do not hesitate to make the social, employment and architectural environment accessible to the physically handicapped; we should recognize our obligations to make the environment equally friendly to people with schizophrenia.

Intervention no. 3

Cognitive-behavioral therapy for psychotic symptoms

We should invest in helping people with schizophrenia develop coping strategies designed to minimize stress and psychotic symptoms, and which may, as a result, eventually allow treatment with lower doses of medication.

Despite the long-held belief that it is a pointless exercise to try and dissuade people from tenacious delusional beliefs, recent research reveals that talking to people about their psychotic symptoms, and about their meaning to the individual, can lead to an improvement in symptoms. It emerges that the gentle challenge of evidence used by people with psychotic disorders to support their delusions – for example, presenting alternative viewpoints, reality-testing and enhancing coping strategies – can be helpful.

In a British study conducted by Nicholas Tarrier and associates (Tarrier *et al.*, 1993), people with schizophrenia who continued to experience positive symptoms of psychosis, despite optimal drug treatment, improved when they received a cognitive-behavioral treatment called coping strategy enhancement. In this approach, patients were helped to identify coping strategies that could be used to reduce both the cues and reactions to symptoms like hallucinations or delusions. For one person, for example, being alone or bored may be a cue to an increase in hallucinations; he or she can be taught to adopt strategies to reduce isolation or boredom. Others can learn to reduce auditory hallucinations by humming, conversing with others, or even reasoning with the voices and telling them to go away and come back later. Similarly, a person might be taught to test the reality of delusional beliefs against the therapist's interpretation of events and, for example, return to a church social group about which he or she had harbored paranoid fears. After six months, the patients who received this type of coping strategy treatment had lower levels of delusions and anxiety, compared to those who received a less specific form of cognitive therapy called problem-solving training.

However, patients who received problem-solving therapy also improved to a degree, so, in a later study, the researchers combined both of these cognitive approaches with a third, called relapse prevention, in an attempt to maximize benefits. One year after the end of the treatment, patients receiving this cognitive-behavioral therapy were experiencing significantly lower levels of positive symptoms than a control group of patients who received routine care (Tarrier *et al.*, 1999).

Another randomized study of cognitive-behavioral therapy for people with persistent symptoms of schizophrenia, conducted at three centers in East Anglia and London, achieved a 25 per cent reduction in total psychopathology, primarily in hallucinations and delusions (Kuipers *et al.*, 1997). In this study, about half of those with persistent symptoms appeared to show benefit from cognitive therapy, primarily those with persistent delusions who initially accepted, to a degree at least, that they might be mistaken in their beliefs (Garety *et al.*, 1998). Benefits for these patients were sustained over a long period and the treatment led to eventual cost savings due to a reduced need for services in the months following treatment (Kuipers *et al.*, 1998).

A study conducted in London demonstrated that cognitive-behavioral therapy provided in group therapy format to people with persistent psychotic symptoms is as effective in teaching coping strategies and giving people control over their hallucinations as is individual cognitive therapy, while being considerably less expensive. Participants in group treatment found that discussing their voices was helpful; many felt comforted by sharing their experience and appreciated learning new coping strategies (Wykes *et al.*, 1999).

Cognitive therapy, it appears, is also effective for patients in an episode of acute psychosis, speeding up the resolution of positive symptoms. Patients in inpatient treatment for an acute psychotic illness (excluding bipolar disorder), in Birmingham, England, were provided with individual and group cognitive therapy, using four procedures in stages during the hospital stay. The individual treatment gently challenged and tested key delusional beliefs. The group therapy consisted of meetings of up to six inpatients in which group members offered alternative explanations for the irrational beliefs of others, challenged negative beliefs about psychotic illness, and bolstered one another's attempts to integrate the concept of illness into their lives and to develop new coping strategies. The other cognitive procedures were family sessions to enlist family support in the patient's attempts to manage his or her symptoms, and an activity program aimed at improving interpersonal and self-care skills. Positive symptoms decreased faster and dropped to a lower level of severity in patients who received the cognitive therapy than in a control group receiving a similar amount of non-specific therapist support and structured activities. The cognitive interventions also appeared to lead to improvements in insight and unhappiness. The authors of the study conclude that the treatment of acute psychosis should include not only medication but also cognitive therapy and efforts to enhance the self-esteem of the acutely ill person (Drury *et al.*, 1996a, 1996b).

Cognitive strategies such as those described here can lead to a reduction in stress levels for people with schizophrenia, by helping them cope better with the stress of the external environment and with the provocations of internal hallucinations and delusional beliefs. The primary cost in providing this type of treatment is in training staff in the methods used; beyond that, additional costs will be low as current staff time can be re-channeled into providing this approach to care. In the US, where cognitive therapy is moderately well-diffused and understood for the treatment of non-psychotic disorders, the approach has scarcely been used with people with psychotic disorders. The opportunity for change and benefit, in enhancing the capacity of people with serious mental illness to improve their ability to cope with their illness, is very great.

Intervention no. 4

Use benzodiazepines to reduce stress-induced psychotic symptoms

We should use benzodiazepines to reduce the effect of stress, rather than increasing antipsychotic drug dosages whenever positive symptoms reappear (Warner, 1994). The belief is widespread in psychiatry (less so now than a decade ago) that the minor tranquilizers, including the benzodiazepine drugs, diazepam (Valium) and lorazepam (Ativan), are harmful or at best worthless in psychosis, but this is not the case. For the person whose auditory hallucinations become louder within days of starting a new job, or for someone who becomes more agitated and disturbed in his or her thinking on returning home for the holidays, taking benzodiazepines for a few days or weeks can bring a quick remission of symptoms.

People admitted to inpatient treatment for the treatment of an acute episode of schizophrenia, who may be overactive and excited, or at risk of hurting others, attempting suicide or running away from treatment, may often be helped in the short run by the use of moderate doses of the minor tranquilizers in addition to antipsychotic medication. These drugs are often effective in calming people with an agitated psychosis – more immediately so, in fact, than the antipsychotic drugs. As a result the psychiatrist can prescribe more modest doses of antipsychotic medication – no more than the amount usually needed for the person to function as an outpatient – and uncomfortable side effects can be minimized.

In some cases, particularly in catatonic schizophrenia, the benzo-diazepines can even have a prompt antipsychotic action. The effectiveness of the benzodiazepines in such cases is probably due to a reduction in the patient's level of arousal. It is also likely that the benzodiazepines exert an antipsychotic effect by their action in blocking dopamine release. They may achieve this effect by stimulating a feedback loop or interneuron in which the neurotransmitter is gamma-amino butyric acid which damps down the release of dopamine (Nestoros, 1980; Warner, 1994) (see the section on the brain in schizophrenia in the Introduction). Several reports have shown that the benzodiazepines in moderate or high doses, alone or in combination with antipsychotic drugs, are effective in controlling psychotic symptoms; somewhat fewer studies have found them to be ineffective or to produce equivocal results (Warner, 1994). On balance, it appears that the benzodiazepines are sometimes effective over longer periods of time for people with schizophrenia but, without doubt, they are most useful in calming the acutely disturbed patient.

An advantage of the benzodiazepines is that they are more pleasant to take than the antipsychotic drugs, especially the older, standard antipsychotics, and are generally free from serious side effects. A disadvantage is that tolerance appears to develop to the antipsychotic action of the drugs, rendering them suitable, in most cases, only for short-term use.

Chapter 4

Access to power

Where do we normally find power and influence in life? As consumers, through money; as workers, through competence or positions of authority in the job; as social animals, from our roles as parents, soccer coaches, school board members, and so on, or through our connections to other people with influence; and as citizens, through our rights in a free society. On this scorecard, the mentally ill are some of the least powerful people in society, confronting the restrictions of poverty, unemployment, stigma, discrimination, social exclusion, jail incarceration, hospital admission (see Chapter 7) and even outpatient treatment.

In the US, rates of employment for people with serious mental illness hover around 15 per cent (Anthony *et al.*, 1988; Consumer Health Sciences, 1997; Office of National Statistics, 1995), and most of those employed have entry-level jobs with little or no authority. The large majority of people with schizophrenia in the US subsist on a disability pension which is well below the official poverty level (Polak and Warner, 1996), surviving on the equivalent of the spending allowance of two average American teenagers. A British schizophrenia sufferer points out how poverty can be a barrier to personal advancement:

> While I was living in an aftercare hostel, we were eligible for two or three pounds a week pocket money as our board and food (*sic*) was taken care of. On some days I literally had difficulty finding the few pence required to buy the newspapers which had the job advertisements I was looking for in them.
>
> (Chadwick, 1997, p. 55)

The span of authority that comes with parenthood is rarely available to people with schizophrenia. Men with schizophrenia are one-third as likely to marry as the average man, and women with schizophrenia are half as likely to marry (Gottesman, 1991). As a result, the likelihood of their becoming parents is similarly reduced (Gottesman, 1991). If they do bear children, repeated episodes of illness increase the risk that their ability as parents will suffer and that they will lose the custody of their children.

People with schizophrenia are more than twice as likely as others in the population to be among the 20 million jail admissions each year in the US, so hundreds of thousands of schizophrenia sufferers spend time behind bars each year, and are detained longer than other inmates (Warner, 1994).

Total institutions, like jails and hospitals, strip people of virtually all their power. As one person, hospitalized for the treatment of schizophrenia, complained to his brother,

> "I'm angry because I'm being treated like a second-class citizen – like a subpatient – and always told to wait. I'm treated like a sub*moron*! Like the most important thing in the world is their lunch hours!"
>
> (Neugeboren, 1997, p. 22)

As many as one-third of patients with schizophrenia, even those in intensive community support programs (Warner and Huxley, 1998), may be admitted to hospital in any year.

One of the triumphs of modern community treatment of the mentally ill has been to demonstrate that intensive outpatient case-management programs drastically reduce admission to hospital (Stein and Test, 1980; Mueser *et al.*, 1998; Latimer, 1999) – good news for people with schizophrenia and bipolar disorder, practically all of whom say that they would much rather be out of hospital than in (Warner and Huxley, 1993). Effective relapse prevention programs, however, tend to be quite controlling. In fact, in states in the US where the mental illness statute allows it, these programs may make considerable use of outpatient certification for involuntary treatment (Swartz *et al.*, 1999). Many people with mental illness see involuntary treatment as an abrogation of their human rights (see the website for the US consumer organization MadNation at www.madnation.org). Even for those who are voluntarily in outpatient treatment, there is a danger that their functional incapacity will lead them to be treated by therapists and case managers as less than full adults, in a paternalistic manner which saps their independence and capacity for self-determination.

Thus we see that the usual routes to everyday social authority and control over one's own destiny are often blocked for people with schizophrenia. Just the experience of having one's own subjective experience objectified and seen as an illness can be dehumanizing and disempowering. As one person with schizophrenia writes, "I have spent years of my life as a footnote, a case note, a clinical note, clinging to the understanding that I was a defective biological unit" (Granger, 1994). Factors which exacerbate this feeling of disempowerment are the sense of being misunderstood by the treatment providers or others in one's life, and ignorance about the nature of one's illness and the treatment being provided. Illustrating this point, people with schizophrenia in a study conducted in Colorado rated education about their illness as one of their most acute unmet needs (Warner and Huxley, 1998).

How does disempowerment affect the outcome from schizophrenia? Most professionals would argue that a person needs insight into being mentally ill in order to benefit from treatment. A study of seriously mentally ill people living in the community, conducted by the author and his colleagues (1989), however, found that accepting the label of mental illness, by itself, was not associated with improved functioning; what was required in addition was an internal locus of control – a sense of mastery over life. But it is this very sense of mastery which is stripped away by the experience of being mentally ill and by the stereotype of incapacity and invalidity which accompanies the label "schizophrenia." Conventional treatment programs, with their element of control, do little to help in developing a sense of mastery. Cognitive treatment methods which enhance coping strategies, as outlined in Chapter 3, are better than many approaches in this respect, but more ways are needed to invest people with schizophrenia with power and control.

"Empowerment" is a buzzword used and abused by those at both ends of the political spectrum from fields as diverse as public welfare, housing, health, education, feminist activism, political action and community psychology. Needless to say, the concept lacks clarity, but, in essence, it refers to a process which operates at a personal and political level to give the marginalized and oppressed in society greater control over their own destinies. As health service researcher Cheryl Merzel defines the process,

> The first level is the realization that one deserves to have one's needs met and that one is capable of making decisions in order to fulfill one's needs. The second level is knowing when and how to use this newly discovered voice, and the third is using the voice and wielding power.

(Merzel, 1991, p. 5)

The consumer (or user) movement, which aims to empower people with mental illness at all these levels, is gaining prominence in many parts of the world. A striking feature of the movement in many countries, however, is its degree of fragmentation. Ask different people for a list of important user organizations in Britain, for example, and there will be little overlap between the lists. A social work professor will suggest MIND, SANE, Survivors Speak Out, Making Space, Turning Point and the Zito Trust. A radical activist might include Survivors Speak Out, but will also list the Self Harm Network, the All Wales User Network, the Scottish User Network and the All Ireland User Network. Another advocate might include the Campaign Against Psychiatric Oppression, Voices, the British Network for Alternatives to Psychiatry, Good Practices in Mental Health, the Afro-Caribbean Mental Health Association, and so on.

In the US, two prominent organizations, the National Mental Health Consumer Association and the National Alliance of Mental Patients, vie for membership, sponsor national conferences, send speakers to professional meetings, combat stigma through media presentations and lobby for political objectives. Another national consumer group is the Support Coalition (www.mindfreedom.org), which operates a listserve called Dendron. The National Association for Rights Protection and Advocacy (NARPA) is another web gathering place (www.connix.com/~narpa). Recovery, Inc. is a well-developed organization with local chapters across the country, and the National Empowerment Center (www.power2u.org), operated by well-known figures like Dan Fisher, a psychiatrist and consumer, and Judi Chamberlin, author of *On Our Own*, is another prominent organization. Other consumer organization websites include the National Mental Health Consumer Self-Help Clearinghouse at www.mhselfhelp.org and People Who Net at www.peoplewho.net.

Lacking unified national leadership, some of the strongest US consumer group activity is at a local level. California, Ohio and New York have particularly active consumer groups. Consumers are appointed to the governing boards of many mental health centers, and state regulations in California require that the boards of residential facilities include consumer members. In half of the states in the US, consumers have been appointed to paid positions in the state mental health administrative offices (Geller *et al.*, 1998).

Fundamental philosophical disagreements over such issues as involuntary treatment and the reality of mental illness increase the tendency for splintering among consumer groups. Group leadership by people with schizophrenia is also held back by the fact that most people who develop this disorder do so before they are old enough to have had any experience of how organizations operate. For mental health agencies wanting to collaborate with users and support the empowerment of their clients, the fragmentation of the primary consumer movement is a problem. Organizations of secondary consumers, relatives of people with mental illness (in the US, the National Alliance of the Mentally Ill, and, in the UK, the Schizophrenia Fellowship), are more cohesive national bodies with local chapters, and making contact with such groups is a relatively simple matter. Mental health agencies need an intervention strategy which allows action at a local level when there is not a strong organization of primary consumers.

Intervention no. 5

Consumer involvement at all levels of service provision

To circumvent the roadblocks to power for people with serious mental illness, we should involve and employ consumers at all levels of mental health service provision. In the USA and elsewhere, consumers of mental health services have become increasingly involved in running their own programs. Consumer organizations have set up cooperative housing projects, drop-in centers, support groups, speakers' bureaus, telephone "warm-lines" and a variety of other services.

A program developed by David Sherman and Russ Porter (1991) at the Regional Assessment and Training Center (RATC) in Denver, Colorado, is an outstanding example of consumer involvement. In the Consumer Case Management Aide Training Program, people who have suffered from serious mental illness are trained, through six weeks of classroom education and several months of on-the-job training, to work with other mentally ill people. Graduates earn twenty-one hours of college credit and are hired, at standard rates of pay, as case management aides at community mental health centers in Colorado. They provide a number of services to their clients including applying for welfare entitlements, finding housing, and teaching living skills. After more than a decade of program operation, well over a hundred consumer mental health workers have been placed in employment throughout the service system, providing models for patients and staff alike of successful recovery from mental illness. Two-thirds of the trainees continue to be successfully employed in the mental health system two years after graduation from the training program. Building on the initial success, RATC now trains consumers for other mental health staff positions, such as residential care workers and job coaches for clients in supported employment.

Consumers can be involved in running residential programs. "The Heights" is a cooperative housing program in north Manhattan, in New York City, which integrates mentally ill and mentally healthy residents and employs the residents in the operation of the apartment building. Management responsibilities in this cooperative, which was established by Columbia University Community Services, the mental health agency for the area, are shared between an independent nonprofit housing corporation, which acts as landlord, the residents and the mental health team. Representatives of each of these three bodies form a council which screens and selects new residents and ensures that one-third of the rooms are allocated to people with serious mental illness. The committee also appoints residents to paid positions, such as concierge, in the cooperative.

One consumer action group has opened its own psychiatric clinic. The Capitol Hill Action and Recreation Group (CHARG), in Denver, is a coalition of consumers and professionals which has established a consumer-run drop-in center and a full-scale psychiatric clinic for the treatment of severely ill people. The clinic is directly accountable to an elected consumer board and to a second board comprised of professionals and other interested people. All matters of clinic policy require the consent of the consumer board. CHARG also provides consumer advocates for patients at the local state hospital, in boarding homes and in other locations. The advocates visit the hospital wards, attend treatment planning meetings and accompany clients to court hearings; among other services, they help clients find apartments, apply for public assistance, appeal adverse Social Security rulings and contest involuntary treatment certifications.

It does not require a special program for a mental health agency to involve consumers in delivering treatment. At the Mental Health Center of Boulder County, in Colorado, people with serious mental illness are part of the governing board, several advisory boards and the board of the agency's fund-raising foundation. The center's vocational workshop is being converted into a business enterprise in which the consumer workers have input into and authority over such issues as working conditions, career ladders, fringe benefits and possible profit sharing. Throughout the agency, consumers are employed as case managers, residential counselors, rehabilitation staff, records department and office workers, consumer organizers, research interviewers, and in a variety of positions in consumer-employing enterprises set up by the agency, such as an espresso coffee cart and a property repair business (see Chapter 8). Other mental health agencies have also found the position of peer research interviewer to be one which can be successfully filled by a consumer, even when he or she suffers from persistent psychotic symptoms (Lecomte *et al.*, 1999). Increasingly, the experience of having coped with a serious mental illness comes to be seen as a hiring advantage, similar to being bilingual. At the Mental Health Center of Boulder County most of the entry-level staff position announcements are posted in the lobby of the agency's offices and clients are encouraged to apply. Consumers also work for the mental health center as volunteers – on the speakers' bureau, for example, teaching about mental illness in schools and community groups, reaching out to isolated clients, or in other roles.

Most of the frequently-voiced fears about hiring consumers are not difficult to overcome. Client confidentiality is not an issue if consumer staff are held to the same professional expectations as other staff. Job performance should be completely separated from treatment. Ideally the consumer staff-person will get treatment at a location that is separate from the work site; this is not always possible in small agencies or in rural locations, but, at least, the job supervisor should not be the same person as the worker's treatment provider. Consumer staff treatment records should be kept in a separate locked filing cabinet, and treatment information should not be used by the job supervisor. Consumer staff should be held to the same job standards as other staff by the supervisor, and the consumer staff-person should not use the work supervisor or co-workers for treatment or expect more on-the-job support and counseling than other workers.

Some problems are more difficult. It is not always clear, for example, what allowances should be made on the issue of professional boundaries between staff and clients. Ordinarily, job supervisors would insist that professional staff do not enter into sexual, business, or certain kinds of social relationships with clients, because the staff member's power and influence could create the possibility of exploitation. When the consumer staff-member's social group, however, consists, in large part, of clients of the agency, such a hard-and-fast rule is not possible. Many of these supervisory issues have to be worked out individually, adhering to the principles that any possibility of client exploitation must be avoided, but that the consumer worker cannot be expected to abandon his or her social support system. One of the difficulties which consumer staff encounter is a sense of isolation, and of being different from their co-workers; so the importance of in-group support between consumers and consumer staff should not be underestimated.

There is a healthy debate over whether empowering people to work within the mental health service system is co-opting the voice of radical change, or whether we should, instead, hire consumer organizers who would operate at arm's length from service providers to develop consumer leadership outside the service sector. Fortunately, these are not mutually exclusive options; both can happen simultaneously, if we invest in them.

Involving and employing consumers at every level of the mental health service system reduces the gulf between "us" and "them," enhances sensitivity and respect towards those who are afflicted by illness, and illustrates for customers and staff alike that the goal of treatment is recovery and full participation in society, and that the treatment process is not a one-way service relationship with the inherent implication of unbalanced power. Ideally, and the ideal may be a way off, it will begin to demonstrate for consumer and staff alike (applying Merzel's levels of empowerment) that consumers deserve to have their needs met, that they are capable of deciding how to fulfill them, and that they know when and how to use their voices and how to wield power.

Part II

Domestic level

Chapter 5

Living with family

People with schizophrenia are much more likely to live with their own families in some cultures than in others. A study by the author and his colleagues (Warner *et al*., 1998), for example, found that over 70 per cent of a large sample of people with schizophrenia in treatment with the public mental health system in Bologna, Italy, were living with their family, compared to 17 per cent of a similar (predominantly Anglo-American) sample in Boulder, Colorado. Elsewhere in Italy it is common for a large proportion of people with schizophrenia to live with family; for example, 64 per cent of a sample in Verona (Faccincani *et al*., 1990) and 84 per cent in Genova (Marinoni *et al*., 1996). Within the US there is a wide variation between cultural groups; in a sample of people with schizophrenia in Ohio, 40 per cent of the Euro-Americans were living with a key relative, compared to 85 per cent of Latino patients (Jenkins and Schumacher, 1999).

In the author's American–Italian study, the quality of life of the people with schizophrenia in Bologna was found to be objectively better in a number of ways, compared to those in Boulder, the advantages often being attributable to living with family (see Table 5.1). For example, the average length of time a patient had been living in his or her current accommodation was twenty years in Bologna but only three years in Boulder. We have seen, in Chapter 3, that people with schizophrenia have an exquisite sensitivity to stress. So, the adverse effect of the frequent change of residence (often due to eviction after a relapse) on the course of illness for American patients could be considerable. In addition, people with schizophrenia in Bologna were much more likely to be living in family-owned property (61 per cent versus 8 per cent), while Boulder patients were obliged to spend a large part of their income on rent. Low income and high rents led to many more of the people with schizophrenia in Boulder being dissatisfied with their economic situation.

Table 5.1 Quality of life of people with schizophrenia in Boulder, Colorado, and Bologna, Italy, in 1994–5

	Boulder	Bologna
Objective information		
Accommodation		
With family (%)	17	73
Owned accommodation (%)	8	61
Staff supervised accom. (%)	16	4
Time in present accom. (months)	38	227
Social life		
Married or living with partner (%)	11	28
Daily contact with family (%)	25	70
Visited friend in past week (%)	71	43
Legal		
Accused of a crime in past year (%)	18	4
Work		
Unemployed (%)	56	47
Employed 30+ hours a week (%)	8	23
Income		
Wage per hour (US$*)	4.68	9.38
Earnings a week (US$*)	83	209
Income per month (US$*)	585	721
Subjective information		
Lacks money to enjoy life (%)	72	41
Wants to move but unable (%)	57	31

* Income figures adjusted for current local cost of living using purchasing power parities

More of the people with schizophrenia in Boulder reported unmet needs to do with accommodation, getting decent food and budgeting their money, whereas, in Bologna, these needs were often met by the family. Consequently, the Boulder mental health agency had to commit more resources to setting up supervised accommodation and wrap-around services to meet patients' daily needs for getting food and medical services, budgeting money and monitoring medicine. The Bologna services, on the other hand, were more free to focus on work rehabilitation, and many more of their patients were employed full-time in sheltered and competitive work.

The better income and more stable work and living conditions of people with schizophrenia in Bologna may even have helped them find partners. Nearly 30 per cent of the Italian patients were married or living with a partner, compared to only 11 per cent of the American subjects.

Subjectively, there was a down side to living at home. Those who were living with family, mostly Italian, reported less satisfaction with their span of influence in the home and a reduced sense of well-being, but overall, especially when looking at the objective differences, Italian patients living at home had a superior quality of life.

The difference in living arrangements for people with schizophrenia in Italy and America is a reflection of big cultural differences in the popular attitude towards adult offspring, healthy or disabled, living at home. As one Italian sociologist remarked, "If in the States a young person doesn't want to leave home, everyone wonders what is wrong with the person. Here (in Italy), if a young person wants to leave home, everyone wonders what is wrong with the family" (Bohlen, 1996, p. 1). There is an additional factor, however, a financial one, which may be contributory. Caregivers in Italy, whether they are a parent, a spouse or unrelated to the patient, are provided with a stipend of about $800 a month to help support a mentally or physically disabled person in the household (de Girolamo, 1998).

Although Italians with schizophrenia seem to benefit from living with their families, we have to ask ourselves whether the family itself benefits or suffers from this living arrangement. A number of studies have shown that the caregivers of people with schizophrenia can carry a substantial burden. The burden appears to be greater for family members of people with schizophrenia than with other psychiatric disorders (Jenkins and Schumacher, 1999), and greater if the person with schizophrenia exhibits primarily negative symptoms such as apathy and social withdrawal (Fadden et al., 1987; Provencher and Mueser, 1997). Recent research shows, moreover, that caregivers of people with schizophrenia are more likely to fall ill with infectious ailments; such physical illness in family members is more common when the mentally ill relative exhibits positive symptoms like hallucinations, but the caregiver's objective and subjective burden is greater when the disturbed relative has a high level of negative symptoms and when social supports are weak (Dyck et al., 1999).

The results of a recent study of randomly selected family members of people with schizophrenia in Boulder, Colorado, and in Bologna and Ancona, Italy, give rise to concern (Piccione, 1999). In this study, as in the earlier Boulder–Bologna one, many more people with schizophrenia were living at home in Italy than in Colorado. Nearly all (96 per cent) of the Italian family members surveyed were living with their relative with schizophrenia, whereas less than a quarter of the American family members were living with their disabled relative. The Italian family members were much more likely to report that they had to neglect their normal pastimes because of problems presented by the relative's illness, or that it was difficult to go on an outing away from home, or to get their housework done or to take a vacation (see Table 5.2). More than half of the Italian family members reported that they didn't feel they could bear the situation any longer or that they often cried or felt depressed (compared to 10 per cent of American family members in each case). Five times as many Italian relatives as American said that they felt everything would be all right if it were not for the patient's condition.

Perhaps the most disturbing findings of this study were those which revealed the depth of the negative feelings that the Italian family members held about their relative with schizophrenia. The Italian relative was much more likely than the American to think that the patient was deliberately trying to be a nuisance, or that he or she was not cooperating with the helpers; and was much less likely to feel that the patient had special talents

Table 5.2 Caregiver's perception of burden and of the contribution of the person with schizophrenia to the family, in Boulder, Colorado, and Bologna and Ancona, Italy, in 1998–9 (per cent)

	Boulder	Bologna/Ancona
Perceived sources of help		
Able to ask 3+ friends or family for help	17	46
Confident of immediate professional help	50	23
Caregiver problems due to person's illness		
Had to neglect hobbies	10	54
Difficulty taking outings	3	20
Difficulty working or doing housework	0	11
Feels unable to bear situation	10	54
Frequent crying/depressed	10	65
Feels everything would be OK if not for person's illness	13	65
Perception of person with schizophrenia		
Is trying to be a nuisance	3	11
Is cooperating with helpers	60	27
Has special talents	67	11
Provides emotional support	34	4
Listens and advises	31	11
Provides companionship	52	15
Helps with household chores	30	11

or abilities. The Italian family members were far less likely to feel that the patient made a positive contribution by helping with household chores, by being a good listener and adviser, or by providing companionship or emotional support.

This finding is especially sad, because we know things don't have to be this way. A study from Madison, Wisconsin (Greenberg *et al.*, 1994), found, as we did in Boulder, that a substantial number of American families report getting practical and emotional support from their relative with schizophrenia. In the Madison study, the families were in regular contact with the person with schizophrenia, but, as in Boulder, in less than a quarter of the cases were they actually living together in the same household. In Madison, a majority of the family members referred to the benefits of companionship, reported getting help with cooking and chores, valued the listening and advice, and so on. It appears that, in the case of families and schizophrenia, some degree of distance makes the heart grow fonder.

The Italian families may have had less adequate professional support than those in Boulder and Madison. The Italian family members were much more likely to turn to friends or family in an emergency, whereas the Boulder families felt more confident of getting help from professionals. It is also possible that the Italians, in this case primarily Italian mothers, were more prone to express their feelings and complain than were the Americans.

Whatever the explanation, it seems fairly clear that living at home is a double-edged sword for people with schizophrenia and their families. The person with schizophrenia obtains many objective advantages from living with family, including protection from isolation, poverty, hunger, homelessness, and stressful life disruptions. The person is better integrated into the local community and, in Bologna, at least, more likely to be working. On the other hand, while it is possible for family members to have a positive and rewarding relationship with the person with schizophrenia, some feel burdened and miserable when living with someone with schizophrenia, and are much more negative about the disabled person than are those who can maintain more distance. Is there a way to moderate the costs of caregiving while achieving some of the benefits of family living?

Clearly any effort to help people with schizophrenia stay in the family home must be combined with efforts to help the family's coping capacity. Several studies have shown that families in Britain and America routinely receive little professional advice, support or information (Fadden *et al.*, 1987; Dixon *et al.*, 1999). Other community studies have shown that the provision of professional support is associated with low caregiver burden, stress and health problems (Falloon *et al.*, 1993; Reinhard, 1994). We should view the family as a great environmental asset, and be ready to devote a lot of our resources to strengthening its capacity to provide for disabled relatives. This includes making financial resources available, as in intervention no. 6, which follows (and as is done in Italy), and providing educational and coping supports, as in intervention no. 7. Our cultural upbringing programs us to do what we feel we must do. Until the cultural imperative changes, Italian mothers will care for their offspring with schizophrenia out of a deeply-etched sense of family obligation, and most American parents will insist on their offspring moving out of the home out of a conviction of the importance of independence. But wherever a family is willing to provide help and accommodation for a disabled relative, we should be prepared to recognize this commitment and help make it a positive experience for family members to offer the benefits that are so valuable for the schizophrenia sufferer. Where the family prefers not to be involved in this way, we should be ready to help them gain more separation. Where appropriate, we can try to create the same advantages through adult foster-family living.

Intervention no. 6

Tax-free support payments for caregivers

We should provide a tax-free support payment to families with a person with serious mental illness living in the home, be it the family of origin, a partner, or a foster family.

In the US, for example, we could expand the current adult foster-care provisions (rarely used at the present time for people with mental illness) to provide larger amounts of money to a broader group of eligible recipients. In Colorado at the present time, adult foster-care funds can be used to expand a person's Supplemental Security Income (SSI) from around $500 a month to around $700 a month. The supplement cannot be obtained for people who receive Social Security Disability Income (SSDI), which is about 40 per cent of the seriously mentally ill. A patient who receives the foster-care allowance is allowed to retain $50 pocket money and the remainder is given to the licensed foster-care provider. If this foster-care increment of less than $200 a month were increased to around $400 a month and made available to all people with severe psychiatric disability (regardless of source of disability income), and if it could be used for foster families, caregivers, partners and the family of origin, we would see an increase in the number of mentally ill people who live with their own families and foster families. Similarly, family support payments currently available in Britain on a restricted basis could be made more accessible for the mentally ill.

Foster-family care for people with mental illness has a long and distinguished history, from the fourteenth-century village of Gheel in Belgium (Bromberg, 1975) to the program operated for the past thirty years by Fort Logan Mental Health Center in Denver, Colorado (Warner, 1994). The mental health center in Boulder, Colorado, operates a program, similar to the Fort Logan model, in which some of the agency's most severely disabled clients are placed with families on the understanding that the person can live there as long as the family and client wish. Foster families are found through newspaper advertising, and are screened and supported by a family care coordinator. The patients receive treatment from a mobile community treatment team. The family is reimbursed $850 a month, less than half of which is paid by the patient and the remainder by the mental health center out of general treatment funds. The cost to the mental health center is supportable for seriously disabled clients because it is less than the cost of a modestly staffed group home.

If adult foster-care support payments were expanded as suggested above, patients, families and the treatment system would benefit. The personal income of patients living in foster care or at home would increase substantially as they would no longer be required to spend most of their income on rent and food. They would rise out of poverty and have disposable income for recreation, transportation and vacations. They would be better placed to marry or live with a partner as the support payment would increase the family income. (As noted above, nearly three times as many people with schizophrenia are married or have a live-in partner in Bologna, where such support payments are available, as in Boulder (Warner et al., 1998).) Because of the decrease in isolation, alienation, poverty and daily living stress, which would come with living with a supportive family, patients might well be less likely to use street drugs, to commit crimes of poverty or to suffer relapses of their illness.

The mental health system would benefit from support payments to caregivers by being able to divert resources currently devoted to supported living, wrap-around assertive community treatment, and medication- and money-management into such rehabilitative efforts as clubhouses, supported employment, and family support and education. For people with severe forms of psychosis who require supervised accommodation and daily monitored treatment, in Boulder service costs can exceed $7,000 a month. Family care, however, is the cheapest form of supervised housing available (Warner and Huxley, 1998). Treatment costs could well be halved for any one of these high-cost patients, and the patient's quality of life improved, if he or she were living with a family.

Chapter 6

Domestic stress

The robust results of the "expressed emotion" (EE) research, conducted in several countries in the developed and developing worlds, reveal that people with schizophrenia living with relatives (by birth or marriage) who are critical or over-involved (referred to in the research as high EE) have a much higher relapse rate than those living with relatives who are less critical or intrusive (low EE) (Leff and Vaughn, 1985; Parker and Hadzi-Pavlovic, 1990). High EE relatives also have a higher sense of burden from caregiving (Scazufca and Kuipers, 1996). In conducting this research, the family member's level of expressed emotion is measured by tape-recording a structured interview with the family member in which he or she discusses the person with schizophrenia, and by having a researcher count the number of remarks expressed which indicate criticism, hostility, over-involvement, warmth or positive attributions. A meta-analysis of twenty-six expressed emotion studies of schizophrenia conducted in eleven countries indicates that the relapse rate over a two-year follow-up period was more than twice as high, at 66 per cent, for patients in families which included a high EE relative than in low EE households (29 per cent) (Kavanagh, 1992). Other studies have shown that relatives who are less critical and over-involved exert a positive therapeutic effect on the person with schizophrenia, their presence leading to a reduction in the patient's level of arousal (Tarrier et al., 1979; Sturgeon et al., 1981). In the same vein, people with schizophrenia who see their parents as being affectionate and undemanding have a low relapse rate if they are in contact with their parents, but tend to do poorly and relapse more often if they are not (Warner and Atkinson, 1988).

There is no indication that the more critical and over-involved relatives are abnormal by everyday Western standards. It appears, in fact, that the households where there is more criticism and intrusiveness are those in which the person with mental illness has personality attributes which make him or her more difficult to live with (Warner *et al.*, 1991). It seems likely that the families in which people with schizophrenia do well have adapted to having a person with a psychotic illness in the household by becoming unusually low-key and permissive (Cheek, 1965; Angermeyer, 1983).

Several studies have shown that family psychoeducational interventions can lead to a change in the level of criticism and over-involvement among relatives of people with schizophrenia and so reduce the relapse rate (Falloon *et al.*, 1982; Berkowitz *et al.*, 1981). The benefits of a low-stress household on the relapse rate in schizophrenia appear to be equally as strong as the effect of antipsychotic drug treatment. Someone with schizophrenia who is taking antipsychotic medication and living in a high EE household runs a roughly 50 per cent chance of relapse in the course of a year; if the household can be changed to a low EE environment, the relapse rate drops to 10 per cent or less (Leff and Vaughn, 1981, 1985). Effective interventions provide three basic ingredients: (1) detailed information about the illness for the family and patient; (2) help for the family to develop problem-solving mechanisms; and (3) practical and emotional support (McFarlane (ed.), 1983; Falloon *et al.*, 1984; Leff and Vaughn, 1985; Leff, 1996). Some approaches are more highly structured than others.

In the intervention designed by Julian Leff and Christine Vaughn in Britain (Leff and Vaughn, 1985), which is one of the less structured approaches, the family is given education on the diagnosis, causes, course, and management of schizophrenia. The education is usually provided in the family home and family members are encouraged to ask questions. The family is also invited to join a relatives' group in which high EE relatives can learn directly from low EE family members about how one can cope with the day-to-day problems of living with someone with schizophrenia without becoming excessively critical or over-involved. The family member with schizophrenia is not invited to attend the relatives' group. The family, including the person with schizophrenia, is also offered individual family therapy in which interpersonal problems are discussed.

The psychoeducational method developed by Ian Falloon (Falloon *et al.*, 1984) consists of education about schizophrenia, communication training, a structured problem-solving method, and some other behavioral strategies. The educational material includes information about maintenance medication, side effects, prodromal warning signals of impending relapse, and the risks of street drug use. The communication training looks at the expression of positive and negative feelings in the family, listening skills, and how to ask others for changes in behavior. The structured problem-solving method teaches family members to identify a specific problem, to list alternative solutions, discuss the pros and cons of each solution, choose the best one, implement it and review how it has or hasn't helped.

These family psychoeducational approaches and others, though different in detail, have all proven highly effective in reducing the rate of relapse in schizophrenia. These methods, however, have not been disseminated at all broadly in community psychiatric practice anywhere in the world. The service programs where the full approach is provided routinely to families with schizophrenia are rare and isolated. When a new antipsychotic drug is released, however, if it is effective and low in side effects, it can capture a large market share and be very widely used within months. Why is a psychosocial innovation, like family psychoeducation, so slow to disseminate? Several explanations suggest themselves:

- In some areas, few patients with schizophrenia are living at home (in Boulder, Colorado, at the present time, the proportion has fallen to 10 per cent), so therapists and managers do not see family intervention as being relevant or cost-effective. In much of the world, however, half or more of people with schizophrenia are living with family.
- Some family organizations, like the National Alliance for the Mentally Ill in the US, have opposed the expressed emotion research and family interventions based on it, claiming that it is a stigmatizing concept. The information presented above should make it clear, however, that researchers and therapists are not blaming the family for causing schizophrenia, but are rather offering training in ways to cope better with having a mentally ill relative in the home. There appears to have been a failure in presenting the information to family members in an acceptable way.
- The psychoeducational research results have not been properly disseminated to the people who need to introduce the intervention into practice – social workers, psychologists and nurses – because they have been published primarily in journals read by, and presented at conferences frequented by, psychiatrists.
- The approach is not profit-yielding and is therefore not marketed aggressively like new antipsychotic medications and antidepressants.
- Community psychiatry is too often fragmented and reactive and does not seek innovations which, if used proactively, could reduce cost and improve quality of life.

The following intervention is an attempt to bypass most of these possible hurdles to dissemination.

Intervention no. 7

Marketing the family psychoeducational approach

A governmental health body or an independent foundation could contract with a commercial marketing company (perhaps one that usually works with a major pharmaceutical company) to sell the concept of the family psychoeducational approach to mental health care providers. The company would produce and distribute free manuals, workbooks and interactive CD-Roms describing the treatment, and videos demonstrating the methodology and its cost-effectiveness, and it would fund local continuing education activities devoted to the approach. Using the techniques of pharmaceutical marketing, the company would hire representatives to talk to clinical staff about the quality-of-life benefits for their patients and to administrators about the cost benefits for the agency. The marketing company would send practitioners attractive mailings which would arrive as frequently as do pharmaceutical flyers, and, in the US, it would target large managed-care entities, promoting the notion that subcontracted practitioners should provide cost-reducing family psychoeducation as an element of treatment if they are to be reimbursed for their services. It would also produce informational media targeted to families of the mentally ill to encourage them to request a program of family education, support and problem-solving training.

The annual cost of such a targeted campaign, if it were marketing a new antipsychotic drug, could run anywhere from $2 million to $25 million for a country the size of the US. For a campaign to promote a social intervention with no competing product, the cost would be at the lower end of this range. For example, it would only take a dozen well-trained and well-paid representatives (with performance-based contracts), at a cost of $1.5 million, to make several on-site contacts a year with the managers of every US community mental health center. The cost of equivalent campaigns in Britain or Italy would be less than a quarter of these figures.

The direct costs of the treatment of schizophrenia amounted to more than $17 *billion* in the United States in 1990, $2.5 billion of which was spent on short-term hospital care (Rice and Miller, 1996). A marketing intervention promoting family psychoeducational interventions which cost $2.5 million would only need to produce a 0.1 per cent reduction in hospital use in the first year to be cost-effective. Must we wait until someone can make a profit before we invest in a social good?

Chapter 7

Alienating environments

Decades ago, in the 1950s, when the locus of care was shifting from the hospital to the community, the innovative practitioners of the day found ways to combat what was called at the time the *institutional neurosis* – the posturing, the restless pacing, incontinence and unpredictable violence which were bred by the restrictions, regimentation and emptiness of hospital life. Humanizing the hospital wards and establishing "therapeutic communities," which changed the power relationships between staff and patients and involved patients in ward management, led to a reversal of this institutionally ingrained behavior (M. Jones, 1968; Clark, 1974).

Restrictions, regimentation and emptiness, however, still loom large in the lives of people with serious mental illness, whether they be living in the community or admitted to hospital for the treatment of an acute episode of illness. As a result, the mentally ill are among the most alienated people in our society, daily confronting the key elements of alienation – meaninglessness (see Chapter 8), powerlessness (see Chapter 4), normlessness and estrangement from society (see Chapter 10) and from work (see Chapter 8). Maddi (1981), Yalom (1980) and others describe an existential neurosis presenting as chronic meaninglessness, aimlessness and apathy coupled with boredom, depression and blunted affect. Those who work with people with long-standing mental illness will recognize these features as common among their clients. Many people with mental illness face lives of aimlessness and boredom (see Chapter 8). Depression is also common in schizophrenia; the Iowa record-linkage study (Black *et al.*, 1985) reveals that completed suicide is thirty times the general population rate for men with schizophrenia and sixty times the expected rate in women with schizophrenia – a higher rate even than in affective disorder. It appears that we have traded the earlier *institutional* neurosis for a new *existential* neurosis which similarly stands in the way of recovery from the original psychotic illness. The same active ingredients which proved successful in reversing the institutional syndrome – normalizing the environment, engaging the patient in his or her own treatment (see intervention 5) and creating opportunities for a productive social role (see interventions 9, 10 and 11) – may also prove effective in relieving the effect of the existential neurosis for the patient in the community.

The person with schizophrenia, however, will not benefit much from a normalizing community environment and opportunities for empowerment if, in the hospital, he or she faces the ultimate degradation – being locked in solitary confinement or strapped down with physical restraints. Although restraints and seclusion have been little used in British hospitals in recent decades, their use is still commonplace in the United States. The use of seclusion can run higher than 40 per cent in an acute admission unit in America (Binder, 1979), and the seclusion-room experience can color and dominate a mentally ill person's view of his or her illness. When hospitalized patients in the US were asked to draw pictures of themselves and their psychosis, over one-third spontaneously drew a picture of the seclusion room. Even a year after the hospital stay, the experience of seclusion, with its associated feelings of fear and bitterness, symbolized for many the entire psychiatric illness (Wadeson and Carpenter, 1976).

The use of restraints is also common in the US. During a one-month period in the 1980s, a quarter of all patients evaluated in a psychiatric emergency room in Cincinnati, Ohio, were placed in restraints (Telintelo et al., 1983). On psychiatric wards, the commonest reasons for the use of restraints are not violence but "nonconformity to community rules" (Sologg, 1978, p. 182) and "behavior disruptive to the therapeutic environment" (Mattson and Sacks, 1983, p. 1211).

Even when free of confinement and restraint, psychiatric inpatients in the US are likely to find the doors of the ward locked, with limited opportunities to leave the unit and pursue any of their usual community activities.

Intervention no. 8

Domestic alternatives to the hospital for acute treatment

We can eliminate many of the restrictions of inpatient treatment and normalize the environment for people with mental illness by creating open-door, domestic alternatives to hospital for acute psychiatric treatment. Such settings offer a number of benefits. They provide care which is much cheaper than hospital treatment, less coercive and less alienating, and they produce a different result. People receiving services in a non-institutional setting are called upon to use their own inner resources. They must exercise a degree of self-control, and accept responsibility for their actions and for the preservation of their living environment. Consequently, clients retain more of their self-respect, their skills and their sense of mastery. The domestic and non-coercive nature of the alternatives described here makes human contact with the person in crisis easier than it is in hospital.

Philosophical origins

There are common origins to many of the alternative settings for the treatment of acute mental disorders. Some (for example, Paul Polak's innovative crisis home program) have links to the postwar therapeutic community movement of which British psychiatrist Maxwell Jones was a major force (Jones, 1968). Others, such as Soteria, in California (Mosher, 1995) and in Berne, Switzerland (Ciompi et al., 1995), trace their roots back to the experimental treatment environments of R. D. Laing and his associates in the Philadelphia Association in London in the 1960s (Barnes and Berke, 1972; Sedgwick, 1982). Crisis intervention facilities in the Netherlands were developed in response to the concept of primary prevention of emotional disorder espoused by Gerald Caplan in his 1963 book, *The Principles of Preventive Psychiatry* (Caplan, 1963).

The thread runs back through these revolutionary postwar developments in social psychiatry to an even earlier source – to the successful elements of early nineteenth-century moral management. There are common themes in these alternative treatment programs and in the models, from the nineteenth and twentieth centuries, to which they are linked, which tell us something about the human needs of patients and the nature of the illnesses being treated (K. Jones, 1972; Warner, 1994). Now, as in the moral treatment era, effective psychosocial treatment settings tend to be small, family-style and normalizing. They are open-door, genuinely in the community, and allow the user to stay in touch with his or her friends, relatives, work and social life. They are flexible and non-coercive, and are often based more on peer relationships than on hierarchical power structures. They involve patients in running their own environment and use whatever work capacity he or she has to offer. The pace of treatment is not as fast as a hospital, and the units generally try to provide a quiet form of genuine "asylum."

Cedar House

Cedar House is a large home on a busy residential street in Boulder, Colorado. It was established more than two decades ago as a program of a community mental health center to control ballooning hospital expenses. Inpatient treatment at Cedar House costs half of the daily rate in local psychiatric hospital wards, and it has proved its worth in other ways. Clients and staff like the facility because it is less confining, coercive, and alienating. As a result, clients make an effort to comply with house rules and severely disturbed patients behave less aggressively than they would in hospital. The program is fairly small and, though domestic in style, it is assertively medical in treatment orientation.

Staffed, as one would staff an acute psychiatric hospital ward, with nurses, a psychiatrist and mental health workers, Cedar House functions as an alternative to hospital for the acutely disturbed patients of the Mental Health Center of Boulder County. Like a hospital, it offers all the usual psychiatric diagnostic and treatment services (except electro-convulsive therapy). Routine medical evaluations are performed on the premises; patients requiring advanced medical and neurological investigation, including those with acute or chronic organic brain disorders, are evaluated by consulting physicians in local hospital departments. Unlike a hospital, it is homelike, unlocked and non-coercive.

As far as possible, Cedar House has the appearance of a middle-class home, not a hospital. Residents and staff may bring their pets with them to the house. A bird may be heard singing in one of the bedrooms and a big dog shoulders its way around the house. On winter nights, a fire burns in the hearth. Staff and patients interact casually and share household duties. Residents come and go fairly freely (some attend work while in treatment), after they have negotiated passes with their therapist. Staff must encourage patients to comply willingly with treatment and house rules; no one can be strapped down, locked in or medicated by force. Many patients, nevertheless, are admitted involuntarily to Cedar House under the provisions of the state mental illness statute; they accept the restrictions because the alternative is hospital treatment, which virtually none prefer.

The people who cannot be treated in the house are those who are violent or threatening, who are so loud and agitated that they would make the house intolerable for other residents, or who are so confused that they cannot follow staff direction. The house cannot handle those who repeatedly walk away or clients who are likely to elope and who, as a result, would be likely to harm themselves seriously. Clients who have direct access to guns and present some risk of using them are not admitted.

In practice, just about everybody with a psychotic depression, most people with an acute episode of schizophrenia and many people with mania can be treated in the facility. Some people with adjustment disorders or personality disorders are considered appropriate for admission. Many clients have a dual diagnosis of mental illness with substance abuse. Very few patients, fewer than 10 per cent, need to be transferred to hospital. Cedar House has not entirely replaced locked hospital care, but it provides more than half of the acute inpatient treatment for the mental health center's clients, and could provide an even greater proportion if more beds of this type were available.

Issues that definitely *don't*, by themselves, preclude admission to Cedar House include: (1) severe psychosis; (2) concurrent medical problems; (3) organic brain pathology; (4) suicidal ideas or gestures; (5) age (any age above 16 is acceptable, people over 65 are commonly admitted); (6) social class (although it sometimes takes a while for new upper-middle-class clients and their families to perceive advantages that Cedar House may have over a private hospital setting); (7) ability to pay for treatment (those who have good hospital insurance are no more likely to be admitted to hospital, and those with no insurance are not rejected for Cedar House – care is provided under the center's usual sliding scale and some clients contribute towards their board and rent); (8) unpleasant disposition; or (9) crabs, infectious hepatitis, AIDS or any contagious conditions that can be controlled by standard infectious precautions.

A number of the people treated in Cedar House would be subject to coercive measures, such as restraints and seclusion, if they were admitted to hospital, where such approaches are available and routinely used. The avoidance of coercion is an important benefit of the residential program – important in maintaining the mentally ill person's sense of self-esteem and self-control.

The normalizing treatment style has many of the features of the consumer-empowering therapeutic community approach. Residents take a hand in the day-to-day operations of the household. Every client has a daily chore, and one resident – the chore-leader – supervises the work of others. Higher-functioning residents assist in aspects of treatment and often, for example, escort the more disturbed on trips outside the house when needed. Although the engagement of clients in the management of the household and in the treatment process is empowering, the extent of patient government is limited. This is because the average length of patient stay is brief, and it is necessary for staff to exercise close control over decisions about admission and discharge in order to make room available at all times for new admissions.

Cedar House is busy. Patients are admitted at any hour of the day or night, as in a hospital. All new patients go through a formal admission procedure and are seen by a psychiatrist within twenty-four hours. There are usually about twenty to twenty-five admissions a month. The need to create bed vacancies for the next emergency admission places pressure on staff and patients alike to limit length of stay to a brief efficient period. Most patients stay a week or two but some stay much longer. The occasional person who stays months is generally a high-risk patient, sometimes potentially dangerous, sometimes medically unstable, who proves difficult to place in the community even with extensive supports and elaborate treatment.

An essential initial step in the treatment of those entering Cedar House is the evaluation of the client's social system. What has happened to bring the person in at this point in time? What are his or her financial circumstances, living arrangements and work situation? Have there been recent changes? Are there family tensions? Has the person relapsed more frequently since establishing his or her current living arrangements? From the answers to such questions a short- and long-term treatment plan is developed which will, it is hoped, not only lead to the patient's immediate improvement, but also reduce the chances of relapse after discharge. The goal for all clients is to leave Cedar House for suitable living conditions and coordinated treatment designed to prevent the revolving-door syndrome and provide a decent quality of life. Virtually no one leaves to stay at a homeless shelter.

A distinct advantage of intensive residential treatment over hospital care is that the lower cost allows treatment to proceed at a more leisurely pace. More time can be spent observing the features and course of the person's illness, selecting and adjusting medications, eliminating side effects and evaluating the benefits of treatment.

Safety is an important issue for residents and staff, and every effort is made to ensure that no one becomes aggressive. Crisis intervention techniques are used to de-escalate arguments or acute upsets, and staff members listen carefully to any client who reports that another resident may be becoming dangerous. Agitated clients may be offered medication or hospitalized if necessary. Everyone is expected to treat everyone else with respect. Residents are generally supportive of one another and, along with staff, reinforce a culture of non-violence and safety. The staff work as a team and each has the opportunity and responsibility to give input into treatment planning.

Residential treatment of this intensity requires a staffing pattern similar to that of a hospital. A mental health worker (psychiatric aide) and a nurse are on duty at all times. On weekdays, three experienced therapists with psychology or social work degrees provide services to the residents; they offer psychotherapy, family therapy, help with practical issues like obtaining disability benefits, and they make arrangements for the client's move back to the community. A psychiatrist is present for three hours a day and available by telephone around the clock. A team leader directs the program and a secretarial assistant manages the office work, building repairs and the purchasing of supplies, food and furnishings. Students and volunteers are used in a variety of ways. A part-time cook prepares the meals with help from the mental health worker.

At least two staff are in the house at all times and one is always a nurse. At night, the nurse sleeps, but is available if needed. People of diverse backgrounds are hired who have high professional standards, are bright and flexible, can handle crisis situations and can work under stress. They must be positive and friendly, and good with co-workers; they must enjoy working with the client population and treat them with respect and dignity.

It has turned out to be important that Cedar House was set up in a neighborhood that is partly commercial. Within a few blocks are many community resources that clients use – grocery stores, a post office, a coffee shop, a hospital emergency room, a park and a recreation center. The neighbors have shown little concern, over the years, about the presence of Cedar House. Early on it was necessary to erect a privacy fence around the property and measures are taken to keep the noise down, especially at night, but, for the most part, there have been few complaints.

The staffing of Cedar House imposes relatively high fixed costs which cannot be reduced without significantly altering the nature of the program. The therapeutic design would be improved if there were fewer than fifteen acutely disturbed clients in residence, but this can only be achieved by driving up the per capita daily cost or by reducing staffing to a level which would restrict the severity of the patients who can be treated.

At $200 a day, Cedar House costs half as much as a hospital. Only a small proportion of the actual costs, however, is covered by reimbursement from the client or insurance companies. The program is not considered a hospital and so many insurance companies do not reimburse the treatment at an inpatient rate. Some health maintenance organizations (HMOs), however, appreciate that Cedar House is a bargain when the alternative is expensive hospital care, and reimburse the mental health center for Cedar House treatment at the full rate. Under the recently introduced capitated Medicaid mental health reimbursement mechanisms in Colorado, mental health agencies are finding inexpensive non-hospital settings like Cedar House far more attractive than traditional hospital units. Apart from that, the reason that Cedar House is financially viable is that it offers a treatment alternative for medically indigent clients.

The high fixed costs of Cedar House would be hard to justify for a mental health agency with a catchment area much below 200,000. With this proviso, the Cedar House model is appropriate for both rural and urban settings. The Colorado Division of Mental Health has replicated the Cedar House design in the northern part of the state and on the western slope of the Rockies as closer-to-home alternatives to state hospital admission for far-flung rural areas. Similar acute treatment settings may be found in Vancouver, British Columbia (Sladen-Dew *et al.*, 1995), Washington, DC (Bourgeois, 1995), Trieste, Italy, and elsewhere (Warner, 1995).

Crisis homes

During the 1970s and 1980s, Paul Polak and his associates at Southwest Denver Mental Health Center in Colorado established and operated a revolutionary system of family sponsor homes for the care of acutely disturbed psychiatric patients. This program consisted of a number of private homes where patients were helped through their crises by carefully screened and selected families. A mobile team of psychiatrists, nurses and other professionals provided treatment to the patients placed in the sponsor homes. The program proved to be suitable for the large majority of the agency's acute admissions and helped reduce the daily use of hospital beds to 1 per 100,000 of the catchment area population (Polak *et al.*, 1995).

Southwest Denver Mental Health Center no longer exists as an independent agency and its system of family sponsor homes is no longer in operation. The system, however, became a model for other agencies, including the Dane County Mental Health Center in Madison, Wisconsin (Bennett, 1995). There, more than a dozen family homes provide care to a wide variety of people in crisis, most of whom would otherwise be in hospital; nearly three-quarters of these clients suffer from acute psychotic illness and others are acutely suicidal. About 40 per cent of the clients entering the program are admitted from the community as an alternative to hospital care; 40 per cent are patients in transition out of the hospital; and 20 per cent are people whose clinical condition is not so severe as to require hospital care but who have housing problems or social crises. The average length of stay is only three days.

Violence by people admitted to a crisis home is almost never a problem: this is partly because of careful selection of appropriate clients and partly because clients feel privileged to be invited into another person's home – they try to behave with the courtesy of house guests. For this reason, people with difficult personality disorders seem to behave better in the crisis home than they would in a hospital ward.

The crisis home model has low fixed costs. Consequently, such a program can be established with quite a small number of treatment beds (four to six) without significant loss of cost-efficiency. For rural communities, the model has the advantage that the crisis homes can be widely dispersed, not centrally located like a hospital, making it possible to provide intensive treatment close to the client's home. To be effective, the treatment agency must sustain a high level of commitment to the success of the program. Each foster-care family requires a substantial amount of support from a consistently available professional, and the patients placed in the home need intensive psychiatric treatment from a mobile team of professionals available twenty-four hours a day.

One might imagine that there are few people in the community who would open up their homes to acutely ill people in this way. When a program of this type was launched in Boulder, Colorado, however, through a combination of newspaper articles and advertising, a hundred people called showing an interest in the program in the first month, and half-a-dozen homes were selected within a few weeks.

Conclusion

To be effective, an alternative acute treatment setting should:

- Be small, with a maximum size of around fifteen patients. The size, however, has to be sufficient to maintain cost-effectiveness.
- Cost less than the hospital so that it can pay for itself through hospital savings. Most acute alternatives cost half as much as hospital care or less (Warner, 1995). The lower cost makes possible a greater length of stay, a slower pace of treatment and, quite often, lower doses of medication.
- Provide a full range of psychiatric evaluation and treatment. A psychiatrist should consult frequently, daily for larger settings, and perform an evaluation of all new inpatients within twenty-four hours.
- Avoid inflexibility of rules. A value of the setting is its capacity to adapt itself to individual needs.
- Give staff considerable room for independent decision making (Mosher, 1995; Warner and Wollesen, 1995).

Such settings offer a number of benefits. They provide care which is much cheaper than hospital treatment, less coercive and less alienating. Despite these advantages, there are fewer such treatment settings in the US and Britain than might be expected given the number of patients who can benefit.

Why are there not more such programs? In Britain, Australia and other countries with national mental health programs which are still tied closely to a hospital base, it is necessary to close hospital beds in order to free up the necessary funding – a task which requires protracted bureaucratic negotiations. In the US, where mental health programs are often more independent of government, the task is more feasible, but, until now, health insurance mechanisms have not supported their use. American managed-care providers are becoming aware, however, that non-hospital programs offer cost/benefit advantages. Where Medicaid capitation schemes for the provision of health care are being introduced in many states across the country we can expect to see hospital-alternative settings, with their opportunities for cost saving, become used more frequently in preference to conventional care.

Part III

Community level

Chapter 8

Work availability

Work was a central component of the humane moral treatment approach of the nineteenth century. The superintendent of the Hanwell Asylum in England, for example, believed that proper employment "has frequently been the means of the patient's complete recovery" (Ellis, 1838, p. 197); and Eli Todd wrote to the family of a patient about to leave the Hartford Retreat in Connecticut, in 1830, "I cannot too strenuously urge the advantage and even the necessity of his being engaged in some regular employment" (Braceland, 1975, p. 684). The moral treatment advocates would be distressed at the predicament of the seriously mentally ill in Britain and America today, most of whom have little or nothing to do in their day-to-day lives. In a study conducted in Colorado, in 1994, for example, half of the mentally ill in the community had no more than one hour of structured activity each day (Warner *et al.*, 1994).

Lacking a useful social role, many people with mental illness face lives of profound purposelessness. Psychotic patients, in fact, score lower than any other group on the Purpose-in-Life Test (Robinson and Shaver, 1969). When people in community treatment for psychosis in northern Colorado were interviewed about their lives, their principal complaints were of boredom and (among the men) unemployment – both rated as being much more problematic than psychotic symptoms (Fromkin, 1985). Many professionals suspect that the high prevalence of drug and alcohol abuse among the mentally ill (see Chapter 2) is in part a consequence of the empty lives that many patients lead. In a study of substance use among the mentally ill in Boulder, the author and his colleagues (Warner *et al.*, 1994) found that those with the fewest planned activities were the heaviest marijuana users, giving "boredom" as the primary reason for drug use.

The benefits of employment

Work is central to the development of self-esteem and in shaping the social role of the mentally ill person, and the following economic and societal observations suggest that the availability of employment may be important for recovery from schizophrenia:

- outcome from schizophrenia is much better in the developing world, especially in rural areas where employment in subsistence agriculture is available (World Health Organization, 1979; Jablensky *et al.*, 1992; Warner, 1994);
- in the developed world, outcome from schizophrenia is better among the higher classes in which unemployment rates are low; but, in the developing world, outcome from schizophrenia is better among the *lower* classes which maintain opportunities for employment in subsistence agriculture (World Health Organization, 1979; Warner, 1994).

Clinical research on people with schizophrenia also suggests that work improves outcome from the illness. Several studies have shown that patients discharged from psychiatric hospital who have a job are much less likely to be readmitted to hospital than those who are unemployed, regardless of the patient's level of pathology (L. Cohen, 1955; G. W. Brown *et al.*, 1958; Freeman and Simmons, 1963; Fairweather *et al.*, 1969; Jacobs *et al.*, 1992). In recent years, supported employment has shown itself to be effective in helping patients achieve stable employment without causing any negative effects, and it can lead to reduced frequency of hospital admission and better social functioning, though not usually to improvement in psychiatric symptoms (Bond *et al.*, 1997; Bailey *et al.*, 1998; Lysaker and Bell, 1995).

In general, the research suggests, therefore, that employment leads to better functioning in schizophrenia, though not always to a reduction in illness severity (Warner, 1994). One piece of research which directly addresses the question of the impact of work on people with schizophrenia indicates, however, that work can lead to symptom reduction. In the early 1990s, Morris Bell and his associates placed 150 people with schizophrenia in six-month work placements in a Veterans Affairs medical center in Connecticut and randomly assigned them to either being unpaid or paid $3.40 an hour. As expected, those who were paid worked more hours. In addition, those who were paid showed more improvement in their symptoms – particularly emotional discomfort and positive symptoms, such as hallucinations and delusions – and were less likely to be readmitted to hospital. The more the patients worked, the more their symptoms were reduced (Bell *et al.*, 1996).

Employment rates

Although work appears to have positive effects in schizophrenia, not many sufferers can take advantage of its benefits. For example, in the US only about 15 per cent of people with serious mental illness are employed (Anthony *et al.*, 1988; Consumer Health Sciences, 1997). In Britain, where only 13 per cent are employed (Office of National Statistics, 1995), the situation is similar. Unemployment is such a routine state for people with schizophrenia in many developed countries that professionals often come to think of it as a natural component of the illness. However, when we observe much higher rates of employment for people with schizophrenia in some industrialized countries than in others, we realize that the problem rests not so much in the individual and the illness as in the social context.

For example, employment of mentally ill people is substantially greater in northern Italy than in the US. In a randomly selected group of people with schizophrenia in treatment with the public service system in Bologna in 1994, nearly half were employed continuously over the prior three months, more than one-fifth full-time (thirty or more hours a week) (Warner *et al.*, 1998). In south Verona around the same time, employment of people with schizophrenia was even greater: nearly 60 per cent were employed, more than a quarter full-time (Warner and Ruggieri, 1997). By contrast, in Boulder, Colorado, where employment of the mentally ill is twice the expected US rate, the figures for a similarly selected group of people with schizophrenia were substantially lower – less than 30 per cent were employed and only 8 per cent full-time (Warner *et al.*, 1998).

Why is there such a wide variation between two modern industrialized countries? The answer lies in the opportunities for and obstacles to employment in the different settings. We will first look at the available employment opportunities.

Employment opportunities

In Britain and America the usual spectrum of employment opportunities for people with mental illness, from the most sheltered to the least, includes the following:

- Sheltered workshops. A widely diffused postwar model developed in northern Europe, regarded by many these days as too institutional and segregated. Opponents argue that people placed in these low-demand settings may fail to advance to more challenging work, even though they are capable of doing so. Supporters point out that, for some people with limited functioning capacity, sheltered settings may be the only feasible workplace.
- Supported employment. Transitional and continuous supported employment are American models in which job slots are developed for patients in competitive work settings. Training and support for patients in these jobs are provided by vocational staff known as job coaches.
- Independent employment. People with mental illness find jobs in the competitive workforce, with or without the assistance of vocational staff.

The first and last of these options require little explanation; the second, supported employment, is less well-known and calls for a more detailed description.

Supported employment

Transitional employment programs (TEPs) were originally developed in the 1970s by Fountain House, the psychosocial clubhouse in New York City. Under this model, vocational staff locate jobs in businesses or agencies in the local community. A person with mental illness is trained by a job coach, and placed in one of these positions for a period of, usually, six months. At the end of that period, a new person with mental illness is placed in the job. The worker is supported on the job, to the extent necessary, by the job coach and may attend support meetings or dinner groups on a regular basis while employed. If the patient cannot work at any time, for whatever reason, the job coach will find another client to work that day or will do the job himself or herself. Consequently, the employer gets a good deal. He or she knows that the job, often a high-turnover, entry-level position, will be permanently and reliably filled and that the worker training is done by an outside service.

The principle behind transitional employment is that the person with mental illness learns basic job skills in a "transitional" position which will help the person achieve the ultimate goal – a permanent, unsupported job in the competitive marketplace. In fact, those who work in TEP positions are more likely to secure independent employment (Mosher and Burti,

1989), but, given the extreme sensitivity of people with disorders such as schizophrenia to the stresses of change, it is hard to support the notion that transitional employment is ideally suited to this population. In fact, one of the main reasons that programs such as Fountain House developed the transitional model of employment was that they found it difficult to locate enough jobs and provide support to all of the clients who wanted work.

More suitable for the stress-intolerant person with mental illness is the model of continuous supported employment, originally developed for people with developmental disabilities. This model is essentially similar to the TEP approach, except that the job is permanent. As the worker adjusts to the demands of the position, work supports can be gradually withdrawn and provided to another client, more recently placed in work. As a result the number of supported employment positions can continue to expand over time.

Supported employment offers several advantages. Employment can be designed to meet the needs of each individual client. Job-sharing can be arranged for those who, because of the disincentives in the social security system and the symptom-generating demands of full-time work, prefer to work part-time. Jobs can be sought to match the skills and preferences of individual clients, and, since positions are permanent, a career ladder is possible.

Supported employment programs are ideally run by a psychosocial clubhouse. The clubhouse model, developed by New York's Fountain House and now disseminating broadly throughout the developed world, is a rehabilitation program run conjointly by people with mental illness (who, in this setting, are no longer "patients" but "members") in cooperation with paid staff. Membership is voluntary and clinical service provision is kept separate from the clubhouse environment. The tasks of running the clubhouse are borne by work groups of staff and members.One work group will run the kitchen and prepare meals for the members, another will put out a weekly newsletter and take care of clerical duties, and, where there is a garden, a group will assume horticultural duties. Thus, the clubhouse can provide an opportunity to members for:

- empowerment in social relations;
- expanded social networks;
- an enhanced social environment and improved nutrition (for many of the members are likely to lead isolated lives in single rooms with limited cooking facilities);

- training in a variety of job skills, for example, clerical, computer use and food service;
- assessment of work functioning by job coaches;
- job placement;
- on-the-job support from coaches and group contact at the clubhouse.

Managers of supported employment projects understand that it is not only workers who respond to recognition and support, but also employers. An advantage for many employers of participating in the program is the sense of contributing to the disadvantaged and the community. Each year, the clubhouse and supported employment program in Boulder, Colorado, organizes a "banquet" (provided gratis by a local restaurateur) at which workers, employers and job coaches rub shoulders as they celebrate the contributions of each group. In this way, mental health service providers and the business community see how they can cooperate to the benefit of both.

Can we improve on the usual spectrum of vocational services available in Britain and America for people with mental illness?

Intervention no. 9

Social firms: consumer-employing businesses

Social firms or consumer-employing businesses, common in parts of Europe but little known in the US, may prove to be a viable addition to the approaches described here for expanding work opportunities. In terms of the degree of shelter from the difficulties of the competitive labor market, this alternative falls between the sheltered workshop and supported employment.

Worker cooperatives employing people with mental illness began in Italy in the 1970s and similar enterprises have subsequently been developed in Switzerland, Germany, the Netherlands, Ireland and elsewhere (Warner and Polak, 1995). In Trieste, Pordenone and Palmanova in north-eastern Italy, each business consortium employs a mixed workforce of mentally disabled and healthy workers in manufacturing and service enterprises. In Trieste the businesses include a hotel, a café, a restaurant, a transportation business, a building renovation company and a furniture workshop. In nearby Pordenone, the enterprises include a large cleaning business, collecting money from public telephones, making park furniture, nursing-home aides, home help for the disabled and a horticultural nursery. In Palmanova, by 1998, eleven tourist hotels had been turned into cooperatives, some of the consumer employees living in the hotels rent-free. In Geneva the cooperative ventures include a publishing house, cooperative housing and a café.

Some small and some large, the enterprises compete successfully with local businesses, winning contracts by competitive bid. In Pordenone, about 90 per cent of the work contracts are made with public agencies such as hospitals, schools, the post office and the fire station. In Trieste, about 60 per cent of the contractual work is for public agencies, including the mental health service; but in Geneva, all the contracts are with the community at large.

The cooperatives use varying amounts of public subsidy. In Trieste, in 1994, the subsidy – in the form of direct grants, donated space, and staff time contributed by the mental health service – amounted to about 20 per cent of the total budget, and in Pordenone, to a mere 1 per cent.

In northern Italy the businesses are organized in large consortia and employ substantial numbers of severely mentally disabled clients. In 1994, the production of the Trieste consortium totaled $5 million and, in Pordenone, $7.1 million. In each consortium about half of the regular workers are mentally ill or otherwise disabled, earning a standard, full-time wage. Some mentally ill people work part-time as trainees and receive their disability pension. Unlike most US programs for people with mental illness, the cooperatives advertise widely and have high community visibility. Thus, the scale and social impact of these enterprises exceed the usual achievements of vocational programs.

Social firms in North America and the British Isles

Can mental health agencies in North America and the British Isles develop nonprofit consumer-employing enterprises similar to the continental European models? There are some successful examples. Monadnock Family Services in Keene, New Hampshire, has established a consumer-owned and -managed cooperative with projects that began by buying, renovating and selling houses (Boyles, 1988) and have now moved on to building garden furniture (Silvestri, 1997). An Asian–American mental health clinic in Washington state established a successful consumer-run espresso bar in 1995 (Kakutani, 1998). Virtually all of the vocational programming for mentally ill people in Toronto, Canada, has been converted to the social enterprise model. One such program is a consumer-run courier business, A-Way Express, which operates city-wide. The employees are people with mental illness who use the public transportation system to pick up and deliver packages all over the city, communicating with their dispatch office by walkie-talkie (Creegan, 1995). In Dublin, Irish Social Firms operate a restaurant, a lunch counter, a wool shop and a retail furniture store. Such ventures appear possible in the economic context of North America and the British Isles, but as yet they have been little developed and do not offer work to more than a few of the potential users.

How can their range be expanded? To give a competitive advantage to consumer-employing businesses, contracts with mental health agencies and other public organizations can be developed. New York state agencies, for example, are obliged by the state finance law to purchase new equipment from consumer-employing programs of the Office of Mental Health whenever possible (Surles et al., 1992).

Similarly, a mental health center can shift services that are currently contracted to outside enterprises (such as courier services or secretarial help) to a consumer enterprise. A property repair and maintenance business at the Mental Health Center of Boulder County was created by diverting contracts with private contractors for repair and preventive maintenance of the agency's numerous buildings to a new consumer-employing venture. The business turns a profit (which covers the losses of another consumer-employing business, an espresso coffee cart) and saves the agency money. Other consumers are employed at the agency in the records office, and as research interviewers, vocational and residential staff and mental health workers.

Conclusion

The development of mixed-workforce business enterprises, which have been successful in expanding work opportunities for people with mental illness in many parts of Europe, particularly Italy, may be viable in Britain and North America, particularly if they use the consumption market of people with mental illness – including the provision of psychiatric treatment and related services – to create opportunities for consumer employment.

The ideal vocational rehabilitation system will be one which provides a spectrum of opportunities, from the most sheltered to the most independent. Social firms lie between sheltered workshops and continuous supported employment in the degree to which they provide shelter and support to the employee. Consequently, they enhance the spectrum, helping to create something suitable for all those who would like to work, and making the opportunities as normalizing and as genuinely integrated into the mainstream life of the community as is compatible with job tenure and job satisfaction.

Chapter 9

Economic disincentives to work

Like everybody else, people with psychiatric disabilities balance several factors to optimize their income. The decision to work is based on three counter-balancing factors: (1) the economic return; (2) the stress and effort involved; and (3) the satisfaction derived from the work. The extent to which work is fulfilling depends upon the job and the individual's personal values. Being mentally ill, the effort of working is often particularly great because stress can exacerbate hallucinations or other symptoms. With the added risk of loss of one's disability pension and (in the US) health insurance, the issue of economic return assumes major proportions.

Psychiatrist Paul Polak, and the author (Polak and Warner, 1996), gathered detailed information on income and expenses from people with long-term mental illness living in Boulder, Colorado. They discovered that the income difference between being unemployed and employed, in Boulder, did not offer much economic incentive for mentally ill people to work. The total cash and non-cash income of subjects who worked part-time was only a little more than for unemployed subjects. This was largely because, when patients started to work, many of them lost part of their disability pension (for example, in the case of Supplemental Security Income, 50 cents on the dollar) and many lost part of their rent subsidy (25 cents on the dollar). For the average part-time worker the loss amounted to what economists term an *implicit tax* of 64 per cent on earned income. The situation was better for full-time workers who met an implicit tax of only 23 per cent on their earnings, but, because of the economic obstacles to accepting part-time work, few mentally ill people achieved full-time employment.

How do people with mental illness resolve the issue of economic incentives? Paul Polak and the author (Polak and Warner, 1996) found that patients identified a minimum earnings level – known to economists as the *reservation wage* (Berndt, 1991) – which made work an economically sensible choice. More than three-quarters of the clients they surveyed ruled out the option of taking a minimum-wage job ($4.25 an hour at that time), but 80 per cent would have worked for $6 an hour. If people disabled by mental illness are to advance economically, they need to find jobs that pay above the minimum wage.

In Britain, disincentives to work are worse than in America. British disabled people run the risk of losing all their benefits if they earn as little as £15 ($25) a week (or £45 ($75) of "therapeutic" earnings). A measure introduced in 1992, the Disability Work Allowance, was designed to reduce this obstacle, but another problem, the loss of housing benefits which accompanies increased earnings, virtually eliminates the incentive effect of the Disability Work Allowance. (In October 1999 the Disability Work Allowance was replaced by the Disabled Persons Tax Credit, but any benefit from this change is minimal.) Since a full benefits package, including the disability pension, housing subsidy and free prescriptions, is worth about £13,000 ($22,000) a year, tax-free, and a full-time minimum-wage job yields only £9,000 ($15,000) a year of taxable income, there is little incentive for the mentally disabled to work part-time or full-time.

In Italy, work disincentives are generally less severe than in the US or Britain because Italian patients may usually retain their disability benefits while working. (In fact, this varies a good deal from area to area, as there appears to be substantial variation in the way in which the pension rules are enforced.) Work disincentives are less severe in Greece for a different reason – the disability pension is so low that working is a better option. The Greek disability pension is less than $120 (£70) a month, and a minimum-wage job brings in four times that amount.

What innovations in social policy would help increase employment for people with mental illness? Econometric labor-supply models (Burtless and Hausman, 1978; Moffit, 1990) can be used to forecast the effects of disability pension policy changes on people with mental disability. Such models require the collection of data on work and income from a sample that is large enough to provide examples of people in each defined category of "budget constraint." To apply this method, econometrist Susan Averett, and the author (Averett *et al.*, 1999), gathered economic information from over 200 randomly selected people with psychotic disorders in treatment with the mental health center in Boulder, Colorado.

The most prominent findings from this analysis were that unearned income was a significant disincentive to working or to increasing hours of work, and that the provision of a wage subsidy was one of the most effective ways to boost working hours. In this model, offering a wage subsidy of $2 an hour led to an increase of more than 5 per cent in weekly work hours. In addition, increasing the "earnings disregard" – the amount of money that a beginning worker can earn before losing money from the Supplemental Security Income (SSI) check – was beneficial. Increasing the current earnings disregard under SSI from $65 to $1,000 boosted working hours by 11 per cent. By contrast, changes in SSI regulations to reduce the rate at which the pension was decreased as people increased their hours of work and their earned income (that is, reducing the implicit tax on earned income) were surprisingly ineffective in boosting work hours.

These findings suggest two possible social policy innovations: (1) increasing the amount of earned income that would be allowed before the disability pension is reduced; and (2) providing a wage subsidy.

Intervention no. 10

Modifying disability pension regulations

British and American disability pension regulations should be changed to increase the allowable earned-income level.

In the US, the allowable earned-income level should be increased from $700 under Social Security Disability Income (SSDI), and from $65 under Supplemental Security Income (SSI), to $1,000 or more a month. As recently as July 1, 1999, the earnings disregard under SSDI was increased from $500 to $700 a month. Although this still did not bring mentally ill and other disabled people up to parity with blind people (for whom the earnings disregard has been over $1,000 a month since 1990) (Arnold, 1998), the change has allowed many disabled people to increase their hours of work and income. The effect of the increase has been to allow a person with schizophrenia on SSDI to work more than thirty hours a week for minimum wage, retain the SSDI pension, and thus receive a total monthly income of $1,200 or more. Unfortunately, this leaves people with schizophrenia who receive SSI (and lose 50 cents for every dollar they earn after the first $65) at only 70 per cent of that income for equivalent work. Americans with schizophrenia would benefit from a revision of disability pension regulations that would permit both Supplemental Security Income (SSI) and Social Security Disability Income (SSDI) recipients to earn $1,000 a month before losing their pension. This would allow anyone receiving disability income to work full-time for minimum wage for a total income of over $1,300 a month. In other words, these disabled Americans could rise from below the official poverty threshold to nearly twice the poverty-income level, without encountering disincentives on the way.

The Work Incentives Improvement Act of 1999 addressed the problem that people receiving SSI or SSDI run the risk of losing their health insurance if they return to work. The bill allows such people to continue to be eligible for Medicaid or Medicare government health insurance, but it does nothing to address the issue of lost cash benefits with return to work.

How could the country afford the more comprehensive change in disability pension policy proposed above? Conceivably the plan could pay for itself by encouraging more people to leave the pension rolls and return to work. In 1998, 10.3 million Americans received SSI or SSDI at a cost to the nation of $66 billion. The US Social Security Administration reports that, so severe are the disincentives to work for the disabled in America, that less than a half of 1 per cent of SSDI beneficiaries and no more than 1 per cent of SSI recipients ever leave the disability rolls to return to work. Clearly there is room for improvement which could bring big savings. These would come primarily from the people receiving disability income who have a modestly higher earning potential who, if not constrained by short-term disincentives, would end up working full-time, earning more than $1,000 a month (that is, at a rate of $6.25 an hour or more), and who would drop their disability pension.

In Britain, a recent policy change allows people to work for a year, without disability income, before their pension rights are formally terminated. Such a move does little to address the gross income discrepancy between low-wage workers and pension recipients. The earnings disregard of £15 a week has not increased since 1988; adjusted for inflation, this amount would be over £28 a week or £112 ($180) a month in 2000. Even an increase in the earnings disregard to catch up with inflation would do little to decrease the disincentives. An increase to £150 a week or £600 ($1,000) a month, however, would substantially improve the incentive to work.

The effect of reduced disincentives would be to increase the number of mentally ill people who are working and the number of hours worked, thus improving the person's sense of purpose and decreasing aimlessness, alienation and, possibly, recreational substance use (see Chapter 2). By increasing personal income, the intervention would alleviate poverty, improve living conditions, increase the stability of housing and, as in Italy, allow more people to develop stable partnerships (see Chapter 5).

Intervention no. 11

Wage subsidies

We could provide a wage subsidy to the most seriously disabled mentally ill people and raise earned income above the minimum wage (currently $5.15 an hour in the US). How could it be funded? Under one approach, government pension regulations could be waived to allow payments to be diverted into wage subsidies. Employers would be reimbursed the difference between the worker's rate of production and pay. The US Department of Labor has already established a time-study process which can be used to measure this difference (Roberts and Ward, 1987).

Under some circumstances, it could be feasible to divert funding currently used for treatment services into wage subsidies. In the US, where much of government-funded psychiatric treatment is being converted to a capitated or managed-care funding mechanism, it may become reasonable to use treatment funds for wage subsidies. Under capitated funding, the treatment agency gets to keep any savings resulting from program innovations that reduce costs. For example, a reduction in hospital costs can be directed to community treatment. If increased employment could be shown to improve stability of illness and to reduce treatment costs, then an agency under capitated funding could choose to provide a wage subsidy for its most disabled patients.

Can treatment costs be reduced by employing patients? Psychiatric treatment costs were more than twice as high for the unemployed patients in the study conducted by Paul Polak and the author (Polak and Warner, 1996) as for the part-time employed. This could be explained in a number of ways: (1) unemployed subjects are more disturbed and require closer monitoring; (2) working patients do better because they are employed and need less treatment; or (3) workers have less time to be in treatment. One thing is clear: the cost of outpatient treatment of the unemployed patient is so high in Boulder (around $2,000 a month) that the expense of providing a half-time wage supplement for these clients could be met by a mere 10 per cent reduction in treatment costs. Such a reduction seems possible, purely because the newly-employed client would be at work half the week and less available for treatment. For example, several studies have shown that the time spent in day-treatment programs decreases substantially for patients who transfer to a supported employment program (Bailey et al., 1998) or to other programs with a vocational component (Kirszner et al., 1991; McFarlane et al., 1992; Meisel et al., 1993). Being in a productive role, moreover, could enhance self-esteem and reduce alienation sufficiently that the course of the patient's illness would improve.

As noted above, a number of studies have suggested that work is associated with reduced hospitalization, but research that addresses the question of cost directly is limited. A study conducted in Boulder by the author and his colleagues demonstrated that treatment costs declined progressively over two years in a group of patients who were enrolled as members of a rehabilitation-oriented clubhouse, while these costs remained constant in a matched group of non-clubhouse members. The treatment cost reduction for clubhouse members was restricted to those who were placed in work, suggesting that the savings may well have been a result of employment (Warner *et al.*, 1999). Similarly the treatment costs for clients admitted to Thresholds, the well-known psychosocial clubhouse in Chicago, which has a rehabilitation program with a strong vocational component, were less than three-quarters of the costs for those admitted to a social club with no vocational component (Bond, 1984). In another study, mentally ill clients randomly selected for a program of accelerated entry into supported employment had treatment costs that were less than three-quarters of those for similar clients placed in a gradual work-entry program; the decreased costs of mental health care for the clients who were rapidly employed more than offset the increased costs of the accelerated work program (Bond *et al.*, 1995).

On the other hand, a study which compared treatment costs for clients in the year before and the year after enrollment in a supported employment program showed slightly increased costs after placement in the program; this study, however, did not report the costs for the second year following enrollment in the work program, when the greatest cost advantages might have been realized (Rogers, 1995). Similarly, a study which compared two day-treatment centers – one of which converted its services to provide supported employment placements, dramatically increasing the employment rate of the clients – found that treatment costs decreased slightly for clients in both programs in the first year following the conversion, indicating that the job placement did not save money, but that, at least, people could be placed in work with no increase in costs. Again, no information was provided for the second year after conversion (Drake *et al.*, 1994).

Overall, it appears that placing mentally ill people in work certainly can save money, but doesn't always. To achieve the potential cost benefits of a wage subsidy, it would be important to track costs carefully over an extended period of time and to structure the program in such a way that treatment savings were realized.

Conclusion

The employment of people with schizophrenia in Britain and America is kept unnecessarily low by disincentives in the disability pension schemes. More mentally ill people would be employed, and for more hours a week, if the pension systems were changed to permit an increase in the amount of earned income that could be retained before the disability pension is reduced, or if we provided a wage subsidy to increase the return on work time invested. Further research is needed to demonstrate whether wage subsidies increase employment and decrease treatment costs for some people with serious mental illness, and whether the wage subsidies could be funded out of the treatment cost savings.

Chapter 10

Stigma

> I have often been fraught with a profound guilt over my diagnosis
> of schizophrenia. . . . I had little idea how dehumanizing and
> humiliating the hospital would be for me. . . . I felt that I had partly
> lost my right to stand among humanity . . . and that for some people
> I would be forevermore something of a subhuman creature. . . .
> Mental health professionals often treated me . . . as if I were a
> stranger or alien of sorts, set apart from others by reason of my label.
>
> (American woman with schizophrenia)
> (Anonymous, 1977, p. 4)

With the growth of interest in community psychiatry in the 1950s and
1960s, attention in the industrial world was focused on the question
of the stigma of mental illness. Star (1955), using vignettes depicting
people with psychotic symptoms, conducted a nationwide survey of
members of the American public in 1950 and found the general reaction
to the mentally ill to be negative and poorly informed. Cumming and
Cumming (1957), using the same techniques in 1951, uncovered similar
attitudes among residents of a rural town (which they called Blackfoot)
in Saskatchewan, Canada, and found that the negative attitudes were
untouched after a six-month educational campaign. Following a survey of
residents of the Champaign-Urbana area of Illinois in the 1950s, Nunally
(1961) concluded that the mentally ill were viewed by the general public
with "fear, distrust, and dislike." "Old people and young people," reported
Nunally, "highly educated people and people with little formal training
– all tend to regard the mentally ill as relatively dangerous, dirty,
unpredictable and worthless." They were considered, in short, "all things
bad" (p. 46).

Since that time, discrimination against many minority groups has
receded. The signs in some American swimming pools which read "No

dogs, Jews or colored" have disappeared, but the prejudice against people with mental illness continues. There has been debate in the research as to whether the high levels of stigma attached to mental illness have diminished at all. A number of researchers in the 1960s concluded that the public tolerance of the mentally ill had improved (Lemkau and Crocetti, 1962; Meyer, 1964; Bentz et al., 1969; Crocetti et al., 1971) and, in the late 1970s, twenty years after Nunally's original survey, Cockerham (1981) again analyzed public attitudes towards the mentally ill in Champaign-Urbana and found them to be somewhat more tolerant. Rabkin (1980) argued in 1980 that attitudes had improved but had subsequently reached a plateau. Other researchers, however, found no improvement in popular mental health attitudes between the 1960s and 1970s (Olmsted and Durham, 1976); a second survey of public tolerance of the mentally ill in Blackfoot, Saskatchewan, twenty-three years after the Cummings' original study, revealed that virtually no change had occurred (D'Arcy and Brockman, 1976).

As recently as 1993, public surveys conducted in two English communities revealed a similar failure to identify someone as being mentally ill as in Star's 1950 US study; the authors argued that there was a reluctance to label someone mentally ill because of the negative associations of the term (Hall et al., 1993). The same study revealed that public tolerance of the mentally ill was scarcely better in a district which had been served for ten years by a model community psychiatry program, than in the area which had no such service (Hall et al., 1993; Brockington et al., 1993). Some British studies, in fact, suggest that certain types of discrimination increased in the 1990s (Sayce, 1998).

More positive attitudes towards treatment and community integration were noted in a 1997 survey conducted in England, Scotland and Wales (Market and Opinion Research International, 1997), in which most respondents felt that schizophrenia was treatable, that treatment should be in the community, and that they would willingly work alongside someone with the disorder. Very few, however, would have been willing for a son or daughter to marry someone with the illness.

Misconceptions continue to abound. In Britain, 50 per cent of survey respondents in the mid-1990s believed that setting fire to public buildings was a "very likely" consequence of mental illness (O'Grady, 1996); and, in an American survey, 58 per cent blamed "lack of discipline" as a cause while 93 per cent blamed drug and alcohol abuse (Borenstein, 1992). People with mental illness are more likely to be seen as being responsible for their condition than AIDS patients, the obese or other stigmatized groups (Weiner et al., 1988). Only 7 per cent of a sample of Austrian journalists believed drug treatment to be effective in schizophrenia (Schony, 1999), and only 4 per cent of the general population in Madrid knew that someone with schizophrenia might hear voices (Lopez-Ibor, 1999). Sixty per cent of the general public in Madrid think that people with schizophrenia have split personality (Lopez-Ibor, 1999), but this myth is even held to be true by 22 per cent of *psychiatrists* in Austria (Schony, 1999). Ignorance about the illness does not mean that people would like to know more; 87 per cent of the general public in Austria want to learn nothing new about schizophrenia (Schony, 1999). Family members of people with the illness are often no better informed than the general public; well over half of a sample of family members in Madrid believed that people with schizophrenia should not study, drive or have children (Lopez-Ibor, 1999).

The World Psychiatric Association Programme Against Stigma and Discrimination Because of Schizophrenia (described later in this chapter) lists a number of widespread misconceptions about schizophrenia, including the following:

- Nobody recovers from schizophrenia.
- Schizophrenia is an untreatable disease.
- People with schizophrenia are usually violent or dangerous.
- People with schizophrenia are likely to infect others with their madness.
- People with schizophrenia are lazy and unreliable.
- Schizophrenia is the result of a deliberate weakness of will.
- Everything people with schizophrenia say is nonsense.
- People with schizophrenia are completely unable to make rational decisions about their own lives.
- People with schizophrenia are unpredictable.
- People with schizophrenia cannot work.
- Schizophrenia is the parents' fault.

Media images

> Whenever I turn on the TV or open a newspaper I see journalists describing my illness as if it's a crime.
>
> (Canadian man with schizophrenia)
> (Closer Look Creative, 1999)

Media representations of the mentally ill have shown little improvement since the Second World War. In the late 1970s and early 1980s, US media were still projecting a sensational image of people with mental illness (Steadman and Cocozza, 1978); TV dramas represented the mentally ill much of the time as violent or homicidal (Gerbner et al., 1981). They were often depicted as bizarre in appearance, vacant, grimacing, giggling and snarling. When the Academy Award-winning film *One Flew over the Cuckoo's Nest* was made at Oregon State Hospital in 1975, the producers had the opportunity to use actual hospital inpatients as walk-on actors; they rejected the idea, however, as real patients did not look strange enough to match the public image of mentally ill people (Wahl, 1995).

A US media survey in 1983 (Shain and Phillips, 1991) found the same misconceptions of mental illness reflected as Nunally had found in 1961. In the following years the US lobbying group, the National Alliance for the Mentally Ill, grew in influence and confronted the issue of media coverage, and by 1988 press reporting had improved somewhat; there was less focus on crime, and more on causes of illness and treatment, but dangerousness was still a dominant focus (Shain and Phillips, 1991). A 1993 review of British news coverage revealed that the mentally ill were almost always portrayed in a negative light – as violent criminals, murderers or rapists, and, at best, figures of fun (Barnes, 1993). A 1994 study of British media coverage of mental illness found that accounts of violence outweighed sympathetic reports by four to one (Philo, 1994). Scaremongering by tabloids continues to be common; a recent British headline trumpeted, "Hospital Bungle Released Beast for Sex Spree" (Wolff, 1997, p. 149), and another vilified health services which were ". . . Setting Patients Free to Kill and Rape" (Wolff, 1997, p. 149).

Prejudice, discrimination and stigma

> If I mention schizophrenia, I won't get the job. If I don't tell them and become ill later, I might be fired.
>
> (German woman with schizophrenia)
> (Closer Look Creative, 1999)

People with mental illness are subject to prejudice, discrimination and stigma. The status afforded the mentally ill has been shown to be lower than that of ex-convicts or the developmentally disabled (Tringo, 1970). Even after five years of normal living and hard work, according to one early US survey, an ex-mental patient was rated as less acceptable than an ex-convict (Lamy, 1966). Branded as "psychos" in popular parlance, the mentally ill encounter discrimination in housing and employment (Miller and Dawson, 1965; Wolff, 1997) and generate fear as to their dangerousness (Monahan and Arnold, 1996). A label of mental illness makes it more difficult to find accommodation (Page, 1977); a recent American study found that 40 per cent of landlords immediately reject applicants with a known psychiatric disorder (Alisky and Iczkowski, 1990). Other researchers have demonstrated a similar effect of the label of mental illness on job-seeking (Farina and Felner, 1973). Although public attitudes and knowledge about mental illness in Greece have improved in recent years (Madianos *et al.*, in press), the level of discrimination continues to be high; 42 per cent of the Greek general public would refuse to employ a person with mental illness (although over 90 per cent would employ a physically disabled person), and 36 per cent would not want to live in a neighborhood which included services for the mentally ill (Parashos, 1998).

Citizens fight to exclude treatment facilities and living quarters for the mentally ill from residential neighborhoods, even though group homes for the mentally ill have not been shown to have adverse effects on communities (Boydall *et al.*, 1989). According to a recent survey of the American public (Robert Wood Johnson Foundation, 1990), the "Not in my Backyard" phenomenon is a widespread obstacle to the community integration of people with mental illness. Over two-thirds of a sample of key mental health service providers in Britain reported confronting "Not in my Backyard" campaigns: most thought that these had increased in the 1990s and reported delaying the opening of at least one facility due to community opposition (Repper *et al.*, 1997). Another British study documented that half of the mentally ill people surveyed reported unfair treatment by general health care services, and a similar number reported being subjected to verbal and physical harassment in the community (Read and Baker, 1996). One 71-year-old man reported, "Various gangs in the district call me 'nutter' and spit at me" (Read and Baker, 1996, p. 10).

The agencies serving the mentally ill are tainted by association and mental health professionals themselves sometimes hold attitudes towards mental patients which are similar to those of the general public; they may even be *more* rejecting. In one study, mental hospital staff were considerably less likely than members of the public to take the trouble to mail a sealed, addressed letter which they believed to have been accidentally lost by a mental hospital patient (Page, 1980).

I feel so alone and so ashamed.

(American woman with schizophrenia)
(Closer Look Creative, 1999)

The mentally ill themselves often accept the stereotype of their own condition. Young patients in rural Ireland viewed "spending time in the 'madhouse' . . . as a permanent 'fall from grace' similar to a loss of virginity" (Scheper-Hughes, 1979). A number of studies have shown that psychiatric patients can be as negative in their opinions of mental illness as the general public (Giovannoni and Ullman, 1963; Manis *et al.*, 1963; Crumpton *et al.*, 1967; Kennard, 1974). Some reports, indeed, indicate that people with mental illness are *more* rejecting of the mentally ill than are family members or hospital staff (Bentinck, 1967; Swanson and Spitzer, 1970); although other studies suggest that people with mental illness are less negative about themselves than about mentally ill people in the abstract (Quadagno and Antonio, 1975; Weinstein, 1983). The perception of stigma by people with mental illness is associated with sadness, anxiety, confused thinking, limited social networks and low satisfaction with life (Link *et al.*, 1987; Markowitz, 1998). While treatment of mental illness can lead to symptomatic improvement, the adverse effects of stigma continue to take their toll (Link *et al.*, 1997).

Moderating factors

Some individual factors are known to moderate stigma and improve public tolerance of the mentally ill. Younger and better-educated people are usually more tolerant (Brockington *et al.*, 1993; Wolff, 1997; Rabkin, 1980). Prior contact with someone who suffers from mental illness decreases stigma and fear of dangerousness, as does knowledge of the person's living situation (Penn *et al.*, 1994). Those who do not perceive the mentally ill as violent are relatively tolerant (Link *et al.*, 1987; Penn *et al.*, 1994; Penn and Martin, 1998). Residential facilities for the mentally ill are better accepted in downtown, transient districts with low social cohesion, and less well accepted in single-family neighborhoods (Trute and Segal, 1976).

Stigma in the developing world

People with psychotic disorders in the developing world are often viewed differently by their community. In recent decades, psychiatrists working in developing countries have often noted the low level of stigma attached to mental disorder. Among Formosan tribesmen studied by Rin and Lin (1962), for example, mental illness was free of stigma. Sinhalese families freely refer to psychotic family members as *pissu* (crazy) and show no shame about it; and tuberculosis in Sri Lanka is more stigmatizing than mental illness (Waxler, 1977).

The World Psychiatric Association Programme Against Stigma and Discrimination Because of Schizophrenia has identified a number of factors in the developing world which tend to promote greater tolerance and community support for people with serious mental illness. These include:

- the absence of large-scale institutional care in the traditional mental health care system;
- the rural agrarian nature of the society;
- the strength of the extended family system;
- explanatory models which place the cause of the illness external to the patient;
- the fact that symptoms of psychosis are more readily reversible and outcome from schizophrenia is better in the developing world.

The authors of a World Health Organization follow-up study of schizophrenia suggest that one of the factors contributing to the good outcome from schizophrenia in Cali, Colombia, is the high level of tolerance of relatives and friends for symptoms of mental disorder – a factor which can help the readjustment to family life and work after discharge (World Health Organization, 1979). An Indian five-year follow-up study of people with schizophrenia found that 80 per cent of families preferred that the disturbed family member continue to stay with the family (Indian Council of Medical Research, 1988). Another Indian study found home-based treatment of schizophrenia to be better accepted and less disruptive for families than hospital care (Pai and Kapur, 1983).

The lower degree of stigma in parts of the developing world may be partly a result of different folk-diagnostic practices. Throughout the non-industrial world, the features of psychosis are likely to be given a supernatural explanation; people with these symptoms may be considered to be victims of witchcraft or, conversely, shamans or spiritualists (Warner, 1994). When urban and rural Yoruba, in Nigeria, with no formal education, were shown Star profiles of mentally ill people, only 40 per cent thought that the person with paranoid schizophrenia was mentally ill (Erinosho and Ayonrinde, 1981) (nearly all Americans label this subject mentally ill (D'Arcy and Brockman, 1976)). Only one-fifth of Yoruba respondents considered the person with simple schizophrenia to be mentally ill (three-quarters of American respondents call this person mentally ill). One-third of the Yoruba, moreover, would have been willing to marry the person with paranoid schizophrenia and more than half would have married the person with simple schizophrenia (Erinosho and Ayonrinde, 1981).

When such people are labeled as being "mad," however, the situation changes. When skilled workers from the area of Benin in mid-western Nigeria were asked their opinions about someone specifically labeled a "nervous or mad person," 16 per cent thought that all such people should be shot and 31 per cent believed that they should be expelled from the country. These educated Nigerians conceived of mad people as "senseless, unkempt, aggressive and irresponsible" (Binitie, 1971).

> We can't tell any of our neighbors. It would hurt my sister's chances of getting married.
>
> (Indian woman with schizophrenia)
> (Closer Look Creative, 1999)

There is evidence that the stigma of mental illness is increasing in parts of the developing world with advancing industrialization and urbanization. Early studies in India found high levels of tolerance and sympathy, willingness to interact with the mentally ill, optimism about treatment, and absence of concealment (Sathyavathi *et al.*, 1971; Verghese and Beig, 1974). More recent Indian studies point to decreasing tolerance. A recent survey of public attitudes in New Delhi (Prabhu *et al.*, 1984) concluded that "the mentally ill are perceived as aggressive, violent and dangerous" by city dwellers. "A pervasive defeatism exists about the possible outcome after therapy. There is a tendency to maintain social distance from the mentally ill and to reject them" (p. 12).

In other industrializing parts of the developing world, reaction against people labeled as mentally ill can be extreme. Since the 1980s there has been a vigorous movement in Hong Kong which opposes the placement of psychiatric half-way houses in residential districts. The movement, supported by a political party, is based on a fear of violence by the mentally ill. One half-way house was opposed on the basis that it was too near a butcher's shop where, it was believed, the sight of a meat cleaver would drive patients to homicide. Angry residents even threatened to demolish psychiatric facilities and used video cameras to track the movements of outpatients (Yip, 1998). It is clear that attitudes to the mentally ill vary from culture to culture and are influenced by the label which is applied to the person with psychosis.

Labeling theory

In the early postwar period, research on the stigma of mental illness was fueled by interest in labeling theory. Once a deviant person has been labeled "mentally ill," argued Scheff (1966), society responds in accordance with a predetermined stereotype and the individual is launched on a career of chronic mental illness from which there is little opportunity for escape. There is evidence to support Scheff's position. One study of the attitudes of residents of a small New England town showed that a normal person of an "ideal type" who was described as having been in a mental hospital was socially rejected to a much greater degree than was a person with schizophrenia who sought no help or who instead consulted a clergyman (Phillips, 1966).

In another study (Rosenhan, 1973), normal volunteers presented themselves for voluntary admission to a dozen different psychiatric hospitals with complaints of auditory hallucinations. Every pseudo-patient was admitted and, although they reverted to normal behavior and denied psychotic symptoms immediately upon admission, each one was labeled schizophrenic at the time of discharge. Staff described the normal behavior of the pseudo-patients as if it were pathological. None was discharged in less than a week – one was detained for almost two months. Such studies suggest that patients with schizophrenia may be subject to pressure to conform to stereotypic expectations which could influence their hope of recovery and their behavior.

Critics of labeling theory argue that the approach understates the importance of the initial deviance and of the inherent pathology of mental illness in causing a label to be attached, and that it minimizes the capacity of mental patients to shake off the harmful effects of stigma (Gove, 1975). Of a dozen studies conducted after 1963, assessing the relative importance of the mental illness label versus the person's behavior in determining public attitudes, most found the effect of labeling to be significant but nearly all found the person's behavior to be more potent (Link et al., 1987). Similarly, in a more recent study, knowledge of the symptoms of a person's acute psychotic episode created more stigma than the label "schizophrenia" (Penn et al., 1994).

Regardless of the relative potency of the illness label, patients and families continue to report that stigma is a significant obstacle to community integration (Penn et al., 1994), and it seems likely that labeling has a significant effect in shaping the self-concept, behavior and symptoms of the mentally ill person. Strauss and Carpenter (1981) conclude that:

Labeling is an important variable affecting the course . . . of schizophrenia. . . . Who can doubt the devastating impact on a fragile person of perceiving that the entire social milieu regards him (wittingly or not) as subhuman, incurable, unmotivated, or incompetent to pursue ordinary expectations . . . ? Can we doubt that a deteriorating course of disorder is fostered when fundamental roles are changed by social stigma and employment opportunities become limited?

(p. 128)

How stigma influences the course of illness

How does the stigma of mental illness affect symptoms of schizophrenia and shape the course of the illness? The author has suggested (Warner, 1994) that people who accept the diagnosis of mental illness feel internal pressure to conform to the stereotype of incapacity and worthlessness, becoming more socially withdrawn and adopting a disabled role. As a result, their symptoms persist and they become dependent on treatment and others in their lives. Thus, insight into one's illness may be rewarded with poor outcome.

The author's view is confirmed by Doherty's (1975) study of self-labeling by psychiatric inpatients. Hospitalized patients who accepted that they were mentally ill were rated as showing the least improvement, and those who denied that they were mentally ill did better. A study by the author and his colleagues (Warner *et al.*, 1989) supports this finding. People who accepted that they were mentally ill had lower self-esteem and lacked a sense of control over their lives. Those who found mental illness most stigmatizing had the worst self-esteem and the weakest sense of mastery. The study suggests that patients can only benefit from accepting that they are ill if they also have a sense of control over their lives. Such people are few and far between, however, since a consequence of accepting the illness label is loss of a sense of mastery. Thus, stigma creates a Catch-22 for people with schizophrenia – accepting the illness can mean losing the capacity to cope with it.

Families of people with schizophrenia

We haven't done much entertaining because of this. I'm never quite sure . . . he's so up and down.

(Mother of an American man with schizophrenia)
(Kreisman and Joy, 1974, p. 46)

The stigma which attaches to mental illness also taints the relatives. The general public and mental health professionals themselves often hold negative attitudes towards the relatives of people with mental illness (Lefley, 1987; Mehta and Farina, 1988; Burk and Sher, 1990). Some family members react by talking to no one about the illness for years, not even to close friends. Others respond by withdrawing socially. One-third of the wives of patients in an early US study followed a course of aggressive concealment including dropping and avoiding friends or even moving to a new residence (Yarrow *et al.*, 1955). Thompson and Doll (1982) found a greater tendency to concealment among family members in 1982 than in a similar study conducted by Freeman and Simmons in 1961; and half of the family members of hospitalized psychiatric patients in a recent US study (Phelan *et al.*, 1988) reported some degree of con-cealment, more frequently when the family member was well-educated. Perceived stigma and misconceptions among family members can influence the course of the illness. Family members' unnecessarily pessi-mistic outlook and distress over negative symptoms of the illness (which may be seen as laziness and passive aggression) can lead to criticism, over-control or rejection of affected relatives, which heightens the risk of relapse (Leff and Vaughn, 1985) (see Chapter 6).

> Mum and Dad called me lazy. When I lost my last job they threw me out of the house.
>
> (British man with schizophrenia)
> (Closer Look Creative, 1999)

What can be done to reduce stigma?

Neighborhood campaigns

Surveys of public attitudes reveal negative attitudes but also a reservoir of goodwill towards the mentally ill. When neighbors of a new group home for people with mental illness in south London were surveyed, two-thirds expressed a willingness to help the new facility and showed interest in learning more about mental illness (Reda, 1995). Organizers found that this goodwill could be mobilized by a focused education campaign which encouraged neighbors to initiate social contact with mentally ill residents (Wolff, 1997). During the campaign, informational packets (videotapes and written material) were distributed, and social events and informal discussion sessions were organized. The campaign decreased fearful and rejecting attitudes and increased contacts between group-home residents and their new neighbors. Thirteen per cent of the neighbors made friends with patients or invited them into their homes, whereas no neighbors did so in an area that was not exposed to the educational program (Wolff, 1997). Campaigns which increase contact with patients can be expected to improve attitudes, since personal knowledge of someone with mental illness is associated with greater tolerance (Penn *et al.*, 1994).

Such projects suggest that neighborhood action campaigns are feasible and effective. Can broader social campaigns achieve a similar impact? To answer this question we should look at some of the advances in modern communication technology.

Social marketing

Since the unsuccessful anti-stigma campaigns of the postwar period, public education methods and techniques for health promotion have improved dramatically. Such "social marketing" campaigns, as they are known in the communication field, have been used successfully around the world in reducing infant mortality, AIDS prevention, family planning, improving nutrition, smoking cessation, and a variety of other causes (Rogers, 1995). Carefully designed campaigns can have substantial effects on behavior (Rogers, 1995). Effectiveness is increased by "audience segmentation" – partitioning a mass audience into sub-audiences that are relatively homogeneous – and devising promotional strategies and messages that are more relevant and acceptable to those target groups (E. M. Rogers *et al.*, 1995; Rogers, 1996).

In developing such campaigns, it is important to conduct a needs assessment which gathers information about cultural beliefs, myths and misapprehensions, and the media through which people would want to learn about the topic. The needs assessment method may incorporate focus groups, telephone surveys and information from opinion leaders. A pre-testing mechanism is then established which allows the promotional strategy to be continuously refined (Rogers, 1995). Initially, specific objectives, audiences, messages and media are selected, and an action plan is drawn up. These messages and materials are pre-tested with specific audiences and revised. The plan is implemented and, with continuous monitoring of impact, a new campaign plan is developed and constantly refined.

Health promotion campaigns aim to heighten awareness and to provide information; the former is possible without the latter, but not the reverse. Awareness campaigns need to be supported by an infrastructure which can link people to sources of information and support – for example, a telephone number to call and trained people to respond to the caller. Ideally, the infrastructure should be a central organization with a local network.

Entertainment media, such as popular songs and soap operas, can heighten awareness and provide information, and are especially useful for socially taboo topics such as mental illness. Soap operas have been successful in advancing social messages in several countries. For example, a TV soap opera in China called *Ordinary People*, which promotes smaller family size and AIDS education, began broadcasting in 1995 and will, in due course, reach 16 per cent of the world's population (E. M. Rogers *et al.*, 1995). A radio soap opera encouraging AIDS awareness and family planning gained a wide audience in Tanzania, and was effective in changing attitudes and sexual behavior. Similarly, a TV program centered on a character named Maria and aired in Mexico for forty years has promoted, among other things, adult education (E. M. Rogers *et al.*, 1995).

Focus groups of local experts and representatives of interest groups help generate the "moral messages" for such serial dramas, and scriptwriters develop positive, negative and transitional characters. Transitional characters switch from positive to negative behavior, or vice versa, to illustrate the rewards and consequences of their decisions. Characters are devised to reflect a variety of age ranges of both genders so that listeners can find someone with whom to identify. The approach embraces social-learning theory and the concept that people model their behavior on others.

It is not necessary, however, to create an entirely new popular song or soap opera in order to harness the entertainment media to a social marketing concept.

Intervention no. 12

Lobbying the news and entertainment media

Through advocacy groups, we can educate people who work in the news and entertainment media. Such groups can lobby the entertainment media to include positive characters with schizophrenia with the goal of educating the public and changing attitudes towards the illness. Pure entertainment soap operas, for example, can be adapted to incorporate characters with a social message. In the US, a group calling itself the "Soap Summit" analyzes the content of soap operas (looking at such topics as teenage sexual behavior), lobbies scriptwriters to change the content of their programs to create positive social messages, and measures the impact of their lobbying on soap-opera content. A character with schizophrenia was recently introduced into one of the most widely watched TV programs in Britain, *EastEnders*. The National Schizo-phrenia Fellowship reports that this story-line attracted unprecedented attention and did more to reduce stigma than any number of worthy media appeals. The program humanized the illness, and exploded the myth that schizophrenia means someone has a split personality and/or that it is likely to make someone violent (Frean, 1997). In Australia, a character with schizophrenia was inserted into the TV soap opera *Home and Away* in response to lobbying by a consumer group.

The Australian movie *Shine* is an example of the successful use of a mainstream entertainment medium to heighten awareness and to communicate information about serious mental illness. This Oscar-winning movie conveyed several stigma-busting messages:

• People recover from schizophrenia;
• Most people with schizophrenia can work even if they have symptoms;
• Work helps people recover from schizophrenia;
• People's responses and attitudes towards someone with schizo-phrenia can influence the course of the illness;
• People with schizophrenia can and should be included in the community.

Shine can be criticized, however, for failing to communicate the important message:

• Poor parenting does not cause schizophrenia.

The subsequent public appearances of David Helfgott as a concert pianist around the world have reinforced the positive messages in the movie.

Local and national advocacy groups can also lobby the news and entertainment media to exclude negative portrayals of people with schizophrenia. Such groups are known as "stigma-busters" or "media-watch" groups. The stigma-busting approach calls upon members to be alert to stigmatizing messages in any medium and to respond appro-priately. The National Stigma Clearinghouse, begun in 1990 by the New York State Alliance for the Mentally Ill, is an example of such a program. The Clearinghouse collects examples of negative portrayals of people with mental illness from across the United States, from television, advertising, films and the print media. Members of the organization write to or phone the responsible journalists, editors or others in the media, explaining why the published material is offensive and stigmatizing, and providing more accurate information about mental illness. The group also encourages local organizations to take local action and distributes a monthly newsletter summarizing recent negative media portrayals and the actions taken to inform people at the responsible media source. In this way the group educates other advocates about what kinds of media portrayals to look for and how to correct them (Wahl, 1995).

An example of a successful stigma-busting intervention was the response coordinated by the National Stigma Clearinghouse to the advance publicity for the November 1992 issue of *Superman* comic reporting that the issue would reveal how Superman was to be killed by "an escapee from an interplanetary insane asylum" (p. 145). The Clearinghouse and other advocacy groups lobbied D.C. Comics, explaining that depicting the killer of the super-hero as mentally ill would further add to the stereotype of mentally ill people as evil and violent. When the death issue hit the news-stands the killer was no longer described as an escaped mental patient or a "cosmic lunatic," nor depicted wearing remnants of a strait-jacket (Wahl, 1995).

The National Alliance for the Mentally Ill, in the US, moved to eliminate a similar negative image in 1984, when Hasbro Toys produced, as part of its GI Joe series of action figures, a new villain, Zartan, with two faces and two identities, described on the box as an "extreme paranoid schizophrenic." The National Alliance pointed out to the manufacturer that the toy communicated to children a link between mental illness and criminality and perpetuated the inaccurate perception of schizophrenia as a form of multiple personality. Hasbro withdrew the toy with apologies (Wahl, 1995).

Stigma-busting groups have to tread a narrow line between educating the media about inaccurate, stigmatizing messages, on the one hand, and, on the other, coming across as intolerant nitpickers – between allowing editors and producers to harbor the misconception that their media content is accurate and harmless because they hear no comments from the public, and, conversely, raising fears of censorship by a vociferous minority group. All groups struggling with stereotypic images, be they based on race, gender or disability status, have to cope with these issues of communication style and strategy. Involving a journalist or other communication professional in the media-watch program can help the group achieve the right balance.

* * *

A national anti-stigma campaign

Building on advances in communication technology, the Defeat Depression Campaign was conducted in Britain between 1991 and 1996 with the goals of reducing the stigma associated with depression, educating the public about the disorder and its treatment, encouraging people to seek treatment early, and improving professional treatment expertise. Campaign media directed at the general public included newspaper and magazine articles, television and radio interviews, acknowledgement by celebrities of their own episodes of depression, press conferences, books, leaflets in multiple languages, audio-cassettes and a self-help video. A program to educate general practitioners, which included conferences, consensus statements, practice guidelines and training videotapes, was also launched (Paykel *et al.*, 1997).

The results of the campaign were clearly positive. Knowledge about and attitudes towards depression and its treatment were tested before, during and after the campaign and showed progressive improvement of around 5 to 10 per cent. At all stages of testing, counseling was regarded positively; antidepressants were initially viewed with suspicion, as being addictive and ineffective, but attitudes towards them improved substantially during the campaign. By the end, members of the general public regarded people suffering from depression as being more worthy of understanding and support, and were more likely to acknowledge the experience of depression in themselves and in close friends. They saw depression as more like other medical disorders and were increasingly positive about general practitioners' capacity to treat the disorder (Paykel *et al.*, 1998).

Can such an approach be used even more broadly?

Intervention no. 13

A global anti-stigma campaign

Building on the advances in communication technology, the World Psychiatric Association, in 1997, initiated an educational program on schizophrenia focusing on social aspects of the illness, effective and humane treatment, and rehabilitation. The project aims to reduce stigma and increase awareness of the public health importance of schizophrenia. The program, which is being distributed throughout the world, is sensitive to differences between cultures by combining internationally and locally produced materials. The program is field-testing materials, such as teachers' guides, brochures, posters and an Internet web page, in different settings, and is preparing them in multiple translations (Sartorius, 1997).

The first pilot project of this global campaign was launched in Calgary, Alberta – a city of nearly a million people – in 1997, with the participation of the author as a representative of the global project. The local action committee, made up of representatives of consumer and family organizations, mental health professionals, health policy makers, researchers and representatives of the press and the clergy, selected the following target groups:

- health care professionals, including emergency room personnel, medical students and senior health care policy makers;
- teenagers aged 15 and 17;
- community change agents such as the clergy, business leaders and journalists;
- the general public.

For each target group, messages and appropriate media were selected. In the case of the teenage target group the messages were:

- No one is to blame for schizophrenia (a message about causes).
- People recover from schizophrenia (a message of hope).
- People with schizophrenia are *people* with schizophrenia (a message of humanity and caring).

The media used were:

- A speakers' bureau of consumers, family members and professionals, organized by the local chapter of the Schizophrenia Society (the Canadian national advocacy group), addressed senior and junior high school classes across the region.
- Health teachers in high schools were provided with a well-researched and attractively designed teaching guide on schizophrenia.
- An Internet web page (www.openthedoors.com) was created, with information on schizophrenia (developed by a World Psychiatric Association panel) with access doors for different types of users: teenagers, health professionals, and consumers and family members.
- A competition for high school students to produce anti-stigma materials was launched. The winners received $500 prizes and public recognition at an awards ceremony.
- Posters promoting the campaign and advertising the competition were posted in the high schools.

Outcome results for the teenage campaign were positive. The proportion of students achieving a perfect score in a knowledge test about schizophrenia doubled to nearly 20 per cent. Attitude scores also improved substantially. The proportion of students expressing the least possible social distance improved from 16 to 22 per cent, and the proportion expressing a high degree of social distance fell to less than 10 per cent.

The campaign to target information to journalists was also a success. Positive coverage of schizophrenia and mental illness in the local newspaper, including human interest stories, research advances, treatment options and funding and program needs, increased by 35 per cent in the months following the start of the campaign. Ironically, because of the unfortunate co-occurrence of several major news events involving mentally ill people during this same period, the number of column inches of news coverage with negative content increased by 44 per cent for schizophrenia and 10 per cent for mental illness. These major news events included the arrest and trial of the Unabomber in the US, the shooting of two police officers at the US Capitol, a break-in at the Canadian prime minister's residence, and various much-publicized homicides in Canada and the US. Clearly, stigma-reducing efforts at a local level can be overwhelmed by the actions of a few untreated mentally ill people which get reported at length to hundreds of millions of people in countries spread around the world. What can be done to counter this? Two things, perhaps. Public policy and funding for the treatment of mental illness must be maintained at a level which minimizes the possibility of attention-stealing acts by untreated mentally ill people, and national advocacy groups must work to see that national news coverage of major events is balanced by accurate information about the nature of mental illness and the need for adequate treatment programs.

Campaign activities targeted towards the general public in Calgary included a radio advertising campaign, newspaper stories, news conferences involving people with schizophrenia, and TV coverage of campaign events. Radio advertising was conducted for over a month over five local stations. The following is an example of one of the three thirty-second radio spots:

Dr. Dickson: "My name is Dr. Ruth Dickson and this is the voice of someone who has recovered from schizophrenia."

Michelle: "I heard two voices making derogatory comments towards me, like 'She's stupid, she's dumb. Why doesn't she just kill herself?'"

Dr. Dickson: "She now lives independently, caring for her child, in our community. But often people's fears promote discrimination, deny these people a friend, a family, a job or a decent place to live.

"Schizophrenia is a treatable brain illness. Find out how you can help us treat the people who suffer from it. Call 1-888-685-4004."

A random-digit telephone survey of the general public was conducted before the campaign launch in 1997 and eighteen months later, after airing the radio spots. It was clear that many people heard the radio spots; 28 per cent of those contacted during the second survey reported hearing a radio spot. However, the impact on the general public was negligible. There was no improvement in knowledge or attitudes among those surveyed. In fact, there was a slight worsening of attitudes, perhaps because of the negative news events which had coincidentally occurred during the period of the campaign.

The lesson from this campaign is that efforts targeted to circumscribed groups, such as those directed at high school students and journalists, are more likely to be successful and will be more affordable, than attempts to reach the general public. Efforts to educate the neighbors of new group homes for mentally ill people, as in the program in London described above (Wolff, 1997) (see pp. 96–97), are likely to be successful. Other appropriate target groups might be general practitioners, local police, emergency-room staff, families of people with schizophrenia, landlords, potential employers, and so on. The possibilities are many and will be determined by local needs, but the approach is one which is basic to the concept of social marketing – segmenting the audience into small, relatively homogeneous sub-groups and delivering a well-honed message, relevant to the target group.

The lasting achievements of the Calgary campaign are significant. Schizophrenia is permanently installed as a topic in the health curriculum of most high schools across the district; several local groups are working together to continue to fight stigma; hospital emergency-room standards for the care of mentally ill people, developed by the campaign, are being adopted as a national hospital accreditation standard; the entire province of Alberta and other districts across Canada are mounting similar consumer-driven anti-stigma or educational campaigns; and consumer groups in and around Calgary are providing more education about mental illness in churches and other community groups, and have better links to the local print media, radio and TV.

A stigma-reducing campaign need not be expensive. Many of the interventions used in Calgary were low-cost, and more expensive media, such as radio advertising, were only used to the extent that funding was available. The two-year budget for the Calgary project, including the limited media campaign directed at the general public, was under US$150,000 (plus a good deal of volunteer time). Even if funds had been more limited, it would still have been possible to introduce education about schizophrenia into the high school curriculum, thus reducing the massive ignorance about this condition throughout an entire generation.

Similar local campaigns are feasible in any locality, and advice on how to conduct one is available from the World Psychiatric Association. Those who are interested in launching a similar campaign may contact Professor Norman Sartorius at the World Psychiatric Association Programme to Reduce Stigma and Discrimination Because of Schizophrenia, Hôpitaux Universitaires de Genève, Département de psychiatrie, Belle-Idée, Bâtiment Salève, 2 chemin du Petit-Bel-Air, 1225 Chêne-Bourg, Geneva, Switzerland, for instructions on developing a local program.

Conclusion

Around the world, the stigma and discrimination associated with mental illness are high, although they are less severe in parts of the developing world, where symptoms of psychosis are at times regarded in a more positive light. Postwar attempts to reduce stigma in industrial countries were largely unsuccessful. Media hyperbole, biased reporting and negative attitudes among the general public continue to be major problems.

Modern communication technology offers the possibility of more successful assaults on stigma, and the British "Defeat Depression" campaign and the World Psychiatric Association global campaign to combat the stigma and discrimination associated with schizophrenia are effectively harnessing these approaches.

Summary and conclusions

From the womb to the workplace, the environment shapes schizophrenia. The physical world and human society control how many people will develop the illness and how its course will run. Biological factors are particularly important in establishing the predisposition to the illness; psychological factors, such as the reaction to stress, can trigger the onset; and sociocultural factors, like the domestic environment or stigma, influence its course and outcome.

A biological factor operating in the womb and at the time of birth – complications of pregnancy and delivery – doubles the risk of developing schizophrenia; obstetric complications are an important risk factor because they are common, occurring in up to two-fifths of all births. Schizophrenia, in fact, may be declining in frequency in the developed world because of the improvement in obstetric care since the Second World War. Unfortunately, women with schizophrenia, already at increased risk of having children who develop the illness because of the influence of genetics, are also more likely than other women to experience complications of pregnancy, thus multiplying the risk that their children will develop schizophrenia.

Another biological factor, the abuse of alcohol and street drugs, while it does not increase the risk of developing schizophrenia, can affect the course of the illness. People with schizophrenia are more likely than others in the population to use street drugs, especially hallucinogens and stimulants, and as many as half of all Americans with schizophrenia will abuse substances at some time in their lives. Most begin before their first full-blown episode of illness, perhaps because many of them feel strange or miserable and want to feel better. Although substance abuse is associated with poor outcome in schizophrenia, this may be partly due to the fact that people with schizophrenia who use drugs are more likely to be noncompliant with treatment. Some drugs, like alcohol and stimulants, clearly seem to have an adverse effect, but people with schizophrenia who use marijuana often have less severe symptoms and fewer hospital admissions. It is possible that some people with schizophrenia are able to adjust the dose of marijuana to decrease unpleasant affective symptoms without making their positive symptoms too much worse.

People with schizophrenia seem to be exquisitely sensitive to stress; the life events occurring before episodes of schizophrenia, and possibly triggering the relapse, are milder than those before episodes of other disorders such as depression. Antipsychotic drugs appear to be particularly important in preventing relapse in schizophrenia where people with the illness are exposed to a lot of stress, but of somewhat less importance for those living in circumstances where the stress is milder.

People with schizophrenia are much more likely to live with their own families in some cultures than others. The quality of life of people with schizophrenia who are living at home is often objectively better, in many ways, than for those who are living independently. Living at home, however, can be a mixed blessing. The person with schizophrenia can get advantages from living with family, such as protection from isolation, poverty, hunger, homelessness, and life stresses. Family members, however, can feel burdened, stressed and unhappy when living with someone with schizophrenia, and they may have a more negative view of the disabled person than those who are able to maintain more distance. We need to view the family as an environmental asset, and devote resources to strengthening its capacity to provide support for people with schizophrenia.

This is especially important because people with schizophrenia living with relatives who are critical or over-involved have a much higher relapse rate than those living with relatives who are less critical or intrusive. Family psychoeducational approaches can decrease the level of criticism and over-involvement among relatives of people with schizophrenia, and cut down the rate of relapse. The benefits of a low-stress household on the relapse rate in schizophrenia appear to be comparable to the effect of antipsychotic drug treatment.

The usual routes to ordinary social authority and control over one's life are often blocked for people with schizophrenia. Facing, as they often do, the restrictions of poverty, unemployment, discrimination, social exclusion, jail incarceration, hospital admission and involuntary treatment, the mentally ill are some of the most disempowered in society. Like other marginalized groups, people with mental illness, in recent years, have been seeking empowerment through solidarity. Unfortunately, a striking feature of the consumer movement in many countries is its degree of fragmentation – a problem which restricts their capacity to achieve change.

The mentally ill are also among the most alienated people in our society, every day confronting the elements of alienation – meaninglessness, powerlessness, normlessness and estrangement from society and work. The therapeutic community, a postwar innovation which proved successful in reversing the institutional syndrome of long-hospitalized people with schizophrenia, contained a number of powerful ingredients – normalizing the environment, engaging the person in his or her own treatment and creating opportunities for a productive social role. These same ingredients may also prove effective in relieving the effect of the existential neurosis which adds to the handicap and hardship of people with schizophrenia in the community at the present time.

Work helps decrease the alienation of people with schizophrenia, by providing a social role, by reducing the sense of purposelessness and social estrangement and by boosting self-esteem. The clinical, social and economic research suggests that work is important to the process of recovery from schizophrenia. In the US and Britain, however, only about 15 per cent of people with serious mental illness are employed. An important cause of this low rate of employment is the economic disincentives which prevent many people with mental illness from working; the income difference between being unemployed and employed is often small, and scarcely makes up for the hazards and losses involved in returning to work. The money lost from the disability pension when a disabled person starts working creates an implicit tax which makes working relatively futile.

People with schizophrenia are subject to prejudice, discrimination and stigma. Despite advances made by many disadvantaged groups in recent decades, the prejudice directed against people with mental illness in the Western world continues almost unabated. Misconceptions continue to abound and media representations of the mentally ill have shown little improvement since the Second World War. Citizens fight to exclude treatment facilities for the mentally ill from residential neighborhoods. People who accept the diagnosis of schizophrenia may feel forced to conform to the popular stereotype of worthlessness and incapacity, and so adopt a role of dependency and inadequacy. Stigma thus puts people with schizophrenia in a catch-22 – accepting the illness can mean losing the capacity to cope with it. Modern communication technology, however, can be harnessed to fight stigma and prejudice. In recent years, social marketing campaigns have been used successfully around the world in a variety of causes including AIDS prevention, reducing infant mortality, reducing the consumption of tobacco and fighting the stigma of depression.

Environmental factors such as those discussed here create opportunities for a number of innovations which may reduce the incidence of the illness and improve the situation for sufferers and their families. The interventions suggested in this book are as follows:

- Educate people with schizophrenia, their relatives and physicians about the added risk of schizophrenia from complications of pregnancy and delivery.
- Individualize substance-abuse counseling for people with schizophrenia and be open to the possibility that a substance may be useful.
- Help people with schizophrenia learn to manage stress through cognitive-behavioral therapy.
- Use benzodiazepines to reduce stress-induced symptoms of schizophrenia, rather than increasing the doses of antipsychotic medication.
- Involve and employ consumers at all levels of mental health service provision.
- Provide a tax-free support payment to families with a relative with serious mental illness living at home, be it the family of origin, a partner, or a foster family.
- Contract, through a governmental agency or a private foundation, with a commercial marketing company to sell the family psychoeducational approach to mental health care providers.
- Establish domestic alternatives to hospital for acute psychiatric treatment.
- Create small enterprises to provide opportunities for people with schizophrenia to work in a mixed workforce, and look within the mental health service budget for possible contracts for consumer-employing business.
- Remove economic disincentives to work for people with psychiatric disabilities. For example, in the US increase the allowable earned-income level under SSI and SSDI to $1,000 a month.
- Pay seriously disabled mentally ill people a wage subsidy to raise earnings above the minimum wage.
- Lobby the entertainment media to include positive characters with schizophrenia and story-lines that are sensitive to people who suffer from the illness.
- Combat stigma by developing a local site under the World Psychiatric Association global "Programme to Reduce Stigma and Discrimination because of Schizophrenia."

It is interesting to note that, as we move from the individual level of environmental influences to the community level, fewer of these interventions would be the primary responsibility of mental health professionals (though they could certainly take a role in promoting them). Most of these innovations depend primarily upon the efforts of policy makers and politicians, advocacy groups, communication experts or even business entrepreneurs. The ideas presented here open avenues to a changing world for people with schizophrenia which extend beyond the confines of treatment services, showing how cooperation between different interest groups can achieve far more than our current limited efforts. In Britain or Italy, this book may be of most interest to health policy makers. In the US, which lacks a coordinated national public health structure to advance benefits such as these, these innovations may be of greater interest to advocacy groups. Whichever group takes the lead, it has the capacity to modify the environment of people with schizophrenia, reduce the occurrence of the illness, enhance the quality of life and improve the outcome for sufferers.

Bibliography

Akbarian, S., Vinuela, A., Kim, J. J., *et al.* (1993) Distorted distribution of nicotinamide-adenine dinucleotide phosphate-diaphorase neurons in temporal lobe of schizophrenics implies anomalous cortical development, *Archives of General Psychiatry*, 50, 178–187.

Alisky, J. M. and Iczkowski, K. A. (1990) Barriers to housing for deinstitutionalized psychiatric patients, *Hospital and Community Psychiatry*, 41, 93–95.

Anderson, R. L., Lyons, J. S. and West, C. (in press) The prediction of mental health service use in residential care, *Community Mental Health Journal*.

Andreasson, S., Allebeck, P., Engstrom, A., *et al.* (1987) Cannabis and schizophrenia: a longitudinal study of Swedish conscripts, *Lancet*, ii, 1483–1486.

Angermeyer, M. C. (1983) "Normal deviance": changing norms under abnormal circumstances, presented at Seventh World Congress of Psychiatry, Vienna, July 11–16.

Anonymous (1977) On being diagnosed schizophrenic, *Schizophrenia Bulletin*, 3, 4.

Anthony, W. A., Cohen, M. R. and Danley, K. S. (1988) The psychiatric rehabilitation model as applied to vocational rehabilitation. In Cardiello, J. A. and Bell, M. D. (eds) *Vocational Rehabilitation of Persons with Prolonged Psychiatric Disorders*, Johns Hopkins University Press, Baltimore, pp. 59–80.

Arnold, R. (1998) Employment and disability, *Psychiatric Services*, 49, 1361.

Atkinson, R. M. (1973) Importance of alcohol and drug abuse in psychiatric emergencies, *California Medicine*, 118, 1–4.

Averett, S., Warner, R., Little, J. and Huxley, P. (1999) Labor supply, disability benefits and mental illness, *Eastern Economic Journal*, 25, 279–288.

Bailey, E. L., Ricketts, S. K., Becker, D. R., *et al.* (1998) Do long-term day clients benefit from supported employment? *Psychiatric Rehabilitation Journal*, 22, 24–29.

Barnes, M. and Berke, J. (1972) *Mary Barnes: Two Accounts of a Journey through Madness*, Harcourt Brace Jovanovich, New York.

Barnes, R. C. (1993) Mental illness in British newspapers: or my girlfriend is a Rover Metro, *Psychiatric Bulletin*, 17, 673–674.

Bateson, G., Jackson, D. and Haley, J. (1956) Towards a theory of schizophrenia, *Behavioral Science*, 1, 251–264.

Beck, J. and Worthen, K. (1972) Precipitating stress, crisis theory, and hospitalization in schizophrenia and depression, *Archives of General Psychiatry*, 26, 123–129.

Bell, M. D., Lysacker, P. H. and Milstein, R. M. (1996) Clinical benefits of paid work activity in schizophrenia, *Schizophrenia Bulletin*, 22, 51–67.

Benes, F. M., McSparren, J. M., Bird, E. D., *et al.* (1991) Deficits in small interneurons in prefrontal and cingulate cortices of schizophrenic and schizoaffective patients, *Archives of General Psychiatry*, 48, 996–1001.

Bennedsen, B. E., Mortensen, P. B., Olesen, A. V. and Henriksen, T. B. (1999) Preterm birth and intrauterine growth retardation among children of women with schizophrenia, *British Journal of Psychiatry*, 175, 239–245.

Bennett, R. (1995) The crisis home program of Dane County. In Warner, R. (ed.) *Alternatives to Hospital for Acute Psychiatric Treatment*, American Psychiatric Press, Washington, DC, pp. 227–236.

Bentinck, C. (1967) Opinions about mental illness held by patients and relatives, *Family Process*, 6, 193–207.

Bentz, W. K., Edgerton, J. W. and Kherlopian, M. (1969) Perceptions of mental illness among people in a rural area, *Mental Hygiene*, 53, 459–465.

Berkowitz, R., Kuipers, L., Eberlein-Fries, R., *et al.* (1981) Lowering expressed emotion in relatives of schizophrenics, *New Directions in Mental Health Services*, 12, 27–48.

Berndt, E. R. (1991) *The Practice of Econometrics: Classic and Contemporary*, Addison-Wesley, Reading, Mass.

Binder, R. L. (1979) The use of seclusion on an inpatient crisis intervention unit, *Hospital and Community Psychiatry*, 30, 266–269.

Binitie, A. O. (1971) Attitude of educated Nigerians to psychiatric illness, *Acta Psychiatrica Scandinavica*, 46, 391–398.

Black, D. W., Warrack, G. and Winokur, G. (1985) The Iowa record-linkage study. I. Suicide and accidental deaths among psychiatric patients, *Archives of General Psychiatry*, 42, 71–75.

Bloom, B. (1985) Personal communication.

Bloom, B. L. (1988) *Health Psychology: A Psychosocial Perspective*, Prentice-Hall, Englewood Cliffs, NJ.

Bohlen, A. C. (1996) For young Italians, there's no place like home. In *International Herald Tribune*, Paris, France, March 14, p. 1.

Bond, G. R. (1984) An economic analysis of psychosocial rehabilitation, *Hospital and Community Psychiatry*, 35, 356–362.

Bond, G. R., Dietzen, L. L., Vogler, K., Katuin, C., McGrew, J. H. and Miller, L. D. (1995) Toward a framework for evaluating costs and benefits of psychiatric rehabilitation: three case examples, *Journal of Vocational Rehabilitation*, 5, 75–88.

Bond, G. R., Drake, R. E., Mueser, K. T., *et al.* (1997) An update on supported employment for people with severe mental illness, *Psychiatric Services*, 48, 335–346.

Borenstein, A. B. (1992) Public attitudes towards persons with mental illness, *Health Affairs*, Fall, 186–196.

Bourgeois, P. (1995) Crossing Place, Washington, DC: working with people in acute crisis. In Warner, R. (ed.) *Alternatives to Hospital for Acute Psychiatric Treatment*, American Psychiatric Press, Washington, DC, pp. 37–54.

Bowers, M. B. (1987) The role of drugs in the production of schizophreniform psychoses and related disorders. In Meltzer, H. Y. (ed.) *Psychopharmacology: The Third Generation of Progress*, Raven Press, New York.

Boydall, K. M., Trainor, J. M. and Pierri, A. M. (1989) The effect of group homes for the mentally ill on residential property values, *Hospital and Community Psychiatry*, 40, 957–958.

Boyles, P. (1988) Mentally ill gain a foothold in working world. In *Boston Sunday Globe*, June 5.

Braceland, F. J. (1975) Rehabilitation. In Arieti, S. (ed.) *American Handbook of Psychiatry*, Vol. 5, Basic Books, New York, pp. 683–700.

Brenner, M. H. (1973) *Mental Illness and the Economy*, Harvard University Press, Cambridge, Mass.

Brockington, I. F., Hall, P., Levings, J., *et al.* (1993) The community's tolerance of the mentally ill, *British Journal of Psychiatry*, 162, 93–99.

Bromberg, W. (1975) *From Shaman to Psychotherapist: A History of the Treatment of Mental Illness*, Henry Regnery, Chicago.

Brown, G. W. and Birley, J. L. T. (1968) Crises and life changes and the onset of schizophrenia, *Journal of Health and Social Behavior*, 9, 203–214.

Brown, G. W., Carstairs, G. M. and Topping, G. (1958) Post-hospital adjustment of chronic mental patients, *Lancet*, ii, 685–689.

Brown, G. W., Birley, J. L. T. and Wing, J. K. (1972) Influence of family life on the course of schizophrenic disorders: a replication, *British Journal of Psychiatry*, 121, 248–258.

Brown, V. B., Ridgely, M. S., Pepper, B., *et al.* (1989) The dual crisis: mental illness and substance abuse, *American Psychologist*, 44, 565–569.

Buckley, P., Thompson, P., Way, L., *et al.* (1994) Substance abuse among patients with treatment-resistant schizophrenia: characteristics and implications for clozapine therapy, *American Journal of Psychiatry*, 151, 385–389.

Burk, J. P. and Sher, K. J. (1990) Labeling the child of an alcoholic: negative stereotyping by mental health professionals and peers, *Journal of Studies on Alcohol*, 51, 156–163.

Burtless, G. and Hausman, J. (1978) The effects of taxation on labor supply: evaluating the Gary Income Maintenance Experiment, *Journal of Political Economy*, 86, 1103–1130.

Caplan, G. (1963) *Principles of Preventive Psychiatry*, Basic Books, New York.

Carpenter, M. D., Mulligan, J. C., Bader, I. A., *et al.* (1985) Multiple admissions to an urban psychiatric center, *Hospital and Community Psychiatry*, 31, 397–400.

Carpenter, W. T., McGlashan, T. H. and Strauss, J. S. (1977) The treatment of acute schizophrenia without drugs: an investigation of some current assumptions, *American Journal of Psychiatry*, 134, 14–20.

Chadwick, P. K. (1997) *Schizophrenia: The Positive Perspective: In Search of Dignity for Schizophrenic People*, Routledge, London.

Cheek, F. E. (1965) Family interaction patterns and convalescent adjustment of the schizophrenic, *Archives of General Psychiatry*, 13, 138–147.

Ciompi, L. (1980) Catamnestic long-term study on the course of life and aging of schizophrenics, *Schizophrenia Bulletin*, 6, 606–618.

Ciompi, L., Dauwalder, H-P., Maier, C., *et al.* (1995) The pilot project "Soteria Berne": clinical experiences and results. In Warner, R. (ed.) *Alternatives to the Hospital for Acute Psychiatric Treatment*, American Psychiatric Press, Washington, DC, pp. 133–151.

Clark, D. H. (1974) *Social Therapy in Psychiatry*, Penguin, Baltimore.

Closer Look Creative (1999) Open the Doors. Video for World Psychiatric Association Programme to Reduce Stigma and Discrimination because of Schizophrenia, Closer Look Creative, Chicago.

Cockerham, W. C. (1981) *Sociology of Mental Disorder*, Prentice-Hall, Englewood Cliffs, NJ.

Cohen, L. (1955) Vocational planning and mental illness, *Personnel and Guidance Journal*, 34, 28–32.

Cohen, S. (1960) Lysergic acid diethylamide: side effects and complications, *Journal of Nervous and Mental Disease*, 130, 30–40.

Consumer Health Sciences (1997) *The Schizophrenia Patient Project: Brief Summary of Results – September 1997*, Consumer Health Sciences, Princeton, NJ.

Craig, T. J., Lin, S. P., El-Defrawi, M. H., *et al.* (1985) Clinical correlates of readmission in a schizophrenic cohort, *Psychiatric Quarterly*, 57, 5–10.

Creegan, S. (1995) An investigation of vocational programmes in North America, *British Journal of Occupational Therapy*, 58, 9–13.

Crocetti, G., Spiro, J. R. and Siassi, I. (1971) Are the ranks closed? Attitudinal social distance and mental illness, *American Journal of Psychiatry*, 127, 1121–1127.

Crumpton, E., Weinstein, A. D., Acker, C. W., *et al.* (1967) How patients and normals see the mental patient, *Journal of Clinical Psychology*, 23, 46–49.

Cumming, E. and Cumming, J. (1957) *Closed Ranks: An Experiment in Mental Health Education*, Harvard University Press, Cambridge, Mass.

Dalman, C., Allebeck, P., Cullberg, J., Grunewald, C. and Koster, M. (1999) Obstetric complications and the risk of schizophrenia, *Archives of General Psychiatry*, 56, 234–240.

D'Arcy, C. and Brockman, J. (1976) Changing public recognition of psychiatric symptoms? Blackfoot revisited, *Journal of Health and Social Behavior*, 17, 302–310.

de Girolamo, G. (1998) Personal communication.

Dixon, L., Lyles, A., Scott, J., *et al.* (1999) Services to families of adults with schizophrenia: from treatment recommendations to dissemination, *Psychiatric Services*, 50, 233–238.

Doherty, E. G. (1975) Labeling effects in psychiatric hospitalization: a study of diverging patterns of inpatient self-labeling processes, *Archives of General Psychiatry*, 32, 562–568.

Drake, R. E. and Wallach, M. A. (1989) Substance abuse among the chronically mentally ill, *Hospital and Community Psychiatry*, 40, 1041–1046.

Drake, R. E., Becker, D. R., Biesanz, J. C., *et al.* (1994) Partial hospitalization versus supported employment: I. Vocational outcomes, *Community Mental Health Journal*, 30, 519–532.

Drury, V., Birchwood, M., Cochrane, R., *et al.* (1996a) Cognitive therapy and recovery from acute psychosis: a controlled trial: I. Impact on psychotic symptoms, *British Journal of Psychiatry*, 169, 593–601.

Drury, V., Birchwood, M., Cochrane, R., *et al.* (1996b) Cognitive therapy and recovery from acute psychosis: a controlled trial: II. Impact on recovery time, *British Journal of Psychiatry*, 169, 602–607.

Dyck, D. G., Short, R. and Vitaliano, P. P. (1999) Predictors of burden and infectious illness in schizophrenia caregivers, *Psychosomatic Medicine*, 61, 411–419.

Eagles, J. M. (1991) The relationship between schizophrenia and immigration: are there alternatives to psychosocial models? *British Journal of Psychiatry*, 159, 783–789.

Ellis, W. C. (1838) *A Treatise on the Nature, Symptoms, Causes, and Treatment of Insanity*, Samuel Holdsworth, London.

Erinosho, O. A. and Ayonrinde, A. (1981) Educational background and attitude to mental illness among the Yoruba in Nigeria, *Human Relations*, 34, 1–12.

Faccincani, C., Mignolli, G. and Platt, S. (1990) Service utilization, social support and psychiatric status in a cohort of patients with schizophrenic psychoses: a 7-year follow-up study, *Schizophrenia Research*, 3, 139–146.

Fadden, G., Bebbington, P. and Kuipers, L. (1987) The burden of care: the impact of functional psychiatric illness on the patient's family, *British Journal of Psychiatry*, 150, 285–292.

Fairweather, G. W., Sanders, D. H., Maynard, H., *et al.* (1969) *Community Life for the Mentally Ill*, Aldine, Chicago.

Falloon, I. R. H., Boyd, J. L., McGill, C. W., *et al.* (1982) Family management in the prevention of exacerbations of schizophrenia: a controlled study, *New England Journal of Medicine*, 306, 1437–1440.

Falloon, I. R. H., Boyd, J. L. and McGill, C. W. (1984) *Family Care of Schizophrenia*, Guilford Press, New York.

Falloon, I. R. H., Graham-Hole, V. and Woodroffe, R. (1993) Stress and health of informal carers of people with chronic mental disorders, *Journal of Mental Health*, 2, 165–173.

Farina, A. and Felner, R. D. (1973) Employment interviewer reactions to former mental patients, *Journal of Abnormal Psychology*, 82, 268–272.

Feinberg, I. (1983) Schizophrenia: caused by a fault in programmed synaptic elimination during adolescence? *Journal of Psychiatric Research*, 17, 319–334.

Fioritti, A., Ferri, S., Galassi, L., *et al.* (1997) Substance use among the mentally ill: a comparison of Italian and American samples, *Community Mental Health Journal*, 33, 429–442.

Frean, A. (1997) EastEnders praised for breaking taboo on schizophrenia. In *The Times*, London, May 10.

Freedman, R. (1999) Personal communication.

Freedman, R., Coon, H., Myles-Worsley, M., *et al.* (1997) Linkage of a neurophysiological deficit in schizophrenia to a chromosome 15 locus, *Proceedings of the National Academy of Sciences of the USA*, 94, 587–592.

Freeman, H. E. and Simmons, O. G. (1963) *The Mental Patient Comes Home*, Wiley, New York.

Fromkin, K. R. (1985) Gender differences among chronic schizophrenics in the perceived helpfulness of community-based treatment programs. Department of Psychology, University of Colorado, Boulder.

Fromm-Reichmann, F. (1948) Notes on the development of treatment of schizophrenia by psychoanalytic psychotherapy, *Psychiatry*, 11, 263–273.

Garety, P., Fowler, D., Kuipers, E., *et al.* (1998) London–East Anglia randomized controlled trial of cognitive-behavioral therapy for psychosis. II: Predictors of outcome, *British Journal of Psychiatry*, 173, 420–426.

Geddes, J. R. and Lawrie, S. M. (1995) Obstetric complications and schizophrenia, *British Journal of Psychiatry*, 167, 786–793.

Geller, J. L., Brown, J-M., Fisher, W. H., *et al.* (1998) A national survey of "consumer empowerment" at the state level, *Psychiatric Services*, 49, 498–503.

Gerbner, G., Gross, L., Morgan, M., *et al.* (1981) Health and medicine on television, *New England Journal of Medicine*, 305, 901–904.

Giovannoni, J. M. and Ullman, L. P. (1963) Conceptions of mental health held by psychiatric patients, *Journal of Clinical Psychology*, 19, 398–400.

Goldberg, S. C., Schooler, N. R., Hogarty, G. E., *et al.* (1977) Prediction of relapse in schizophrenic outpatients treated by drug and sociotherapy, *Archives of General Psychiatry*, 34, 297–307.

Gottesman, I. (1991) *Schizophrenia Genesis: The Origins of Madness*, Freeman, New York.

Gove, W. R. (1975) Labelling and mental illness. In Gove, W. R. (ed.) *The Labelling of Deviance: Evaluating a Perspective*, Halsted, New York.

Granger, D. (1994) Recovery from mental illness: a first-person perspective of an emerging paradigm. Presented at the First National Forum on Recovery from Mental Illness, Ohio.

Greenberg, J. S., Greenley, J. R. and Benedict, P. (1994) Contributions of persons with serious mental illness to their families, *Hospital and Community Psychiatry*, 45, 475–480.

Griffiths, R., White, M. and Stonehouse, M. (1989) Ethnic differences in birth statistics from central Birmingham, *British Medical Journal*, 298, 94–95.

Gulbinat, W., Dupont, A. Jablensky, A., *et al.* (1992) Cancer incidence of schizophrenic patients: results of record-linkage studies in three countries, *British Journal of Psychiatry*, 161 (suppl.), 75–85.

Gupta, S. and Murray, R. M. (1991) The changing incidence of schizophrenia: fact or artifact? *Directions in Psychiatry*, 11, 1–8.

Hall, P., Brockington, I. F., Levings, J., *et al.* (1993) A comparison of responses to the mentally ill in two communities, *British Journal of Psychiatry*, 162, 99–108.

Hambrecht, M. and Hafner, H. (1995) Substance abuse or schizophrenia: which comes first? In *World Psychiatric Association Section of Epidemiology and Community Psychiatry Symposium*, New York City.

Hirsch, S. and Leff, J. (1975) *Abnormality in Parents of Schizophrenics*, Oxford University Press, London.

Hoffman, R. E. and McGlashan, T. H. (1997) Synaptic elimination, neuro-development, and the mechanism of hallucinated "voices" in schizophrenia, *American Journal of Psychiatry*, 154, 1683–1689.

Hultman, C. M., Sparen, P., Takei, N., *et al.* (1999) Prenatal and perinatal risk factors for schizophrenia, affective psychosis, and reactive psychosis of early onset: case control study, *British Medical Journal*, 318, 421–426.

Huttenlocher, P. R. (1979) Synaptic density in the human frontal cortex – developmental changes and effects of aging, *Brain Research*, 163, 195–205.

Indian Council of Medical Research (1988) *Multicentred Collaborative Study of Factors Associated with Cause and Outcome of Schizophrenia*, Indian Council of Medical Research, New Delhi, India.

Jablensky, A., Sartorius, N., Ernberg, G., *et al.* (1992) Schizophrenia: manifestations, incidence and course in different cultures: a World Health Organization ten-country study, *Psychological Medicine*, suppl. 20.

Jacobs, H. E., Wissusik, D., Collier, R., *et al.* (1992) Correlations between psychiatric disabilities and vocational outcome, *Hospital and Community Psychiatry*, 43, 365–369.

Jenkins, J. H. and Schumacher, J. G. (1999) Family burden of schizophrenia and depressive illness: specifying the effects of ethnicity, gender and social ecology, *British Journal of Psychiatry*, 174, 31–38.

Jerrell, J. M. and Ridgely, M. R. (1995) Comparative effectiveness of three approaches to serving people with severe mental illness and substance abuse disorders, *Journal of Nervous and Mental Disease*, 183, 566–576.

Johnston, L. D., O'Malley, P. M. and Bachman, J. G. (1989) *Drug Use, Drinking and Smoking: National Survey Results from High School, College, and Young Adult Populations 1975–1988*, National Institute on Drug Abuse, Rockville, MD.

Jones, K. (1972) *A History of Mental Health Services*, Routledge & Kegan Paul, London.

Jones, M. (1968) *Social Psychiatry in Practice: The Idea of the Therapeutic Community*, Penguin, Baltimore.

Jones, P. B., Rantakallio, P., Hartikainen, A-L., Isohanni, M. and Sipila, P. (1998) Schizophrenia as a long-term outcome of pregnancy, delivery, and perinatal complications: a 28-year follow-up of the 1996 north Finland general population birth cohort, *American Journal of Psychiatry*, 155, 355–364.

Kakutani, K. (1998) New Life Espresso: report on a business run by people with psychiatric disabilities, *Psychiatric Rehabilitation Journal*, 22, 111–115.

Kavanagh, D. J. (1992) Recent developments in expressed emotion and schizophrenia, *British Journal of Psychiatry*, 160, 601–620.

Kelly, R. H., Danielsen, B. H., Golding, J. M., *et al.* (1999) Adequacy of prenatal care among women with psychiatric diagnoses giving birth in California in 1994 and 1995, *Psychiatric Services*, 50, 1584–1590.

Kennard, D. (1974) The newly admitted psychiatric patient as seen by self and others, *British Journal of Medical Psychology*, 47, 27–41.

Kirszner, M. L., McKay, C. D. and Tippett, M. L. (1991) Homeless and mental health replication of the PACT model in Delaware. Proceedings of the Second Annual Conference on State Mental Health Agency Services Research, NASMHPD Research Institute, Alexandria, Va., pp. 68–82.

Kreisman, D. E. and Joy, V. D. (1974) Family response to the mental illness of a relative: a review of the literature, *Schizophrenia Bulletin*, 10, 34–57.

Kuipers, E., Garety, P., Fowler, D., *et al.* (1997) London–East Anglia randomized controlled trial of cognitive-behavioral therapy for psychosis. I: Effects of the treatment phase, *British Journal of Psychiatry*, 171, 319–327.

Kuipers, E., Fowler, D., Garety, P., *et al.* (1998) London–East Anglia randomised controlled trial of cognitive-behaviour therapy for psychosis. II: follow-up and economic evaluation at 18 months, *British Journal of Psychiatry*, 173, 61–68.

Laing, R. D. and Esterton, A. (1970) *Sanity, Madness and the Family: Families of Schizophrenics*, Penguin Books, Baltimore.

Lamy, R. E. (1966) Social consequences of mental illness, *Journal of Consulting Psychology*, 30, 450–455.

Latimer, E. (1999) Economic impacts of assertive community treatment: a review of the literature, *Canadian Journal of Psychiatry*, 44, 443–454.

Lecomte, T., Wilde, J. B. and Wallace, C. J. (1999) Mental health consumers as peer interviewers, *Psychiatric Services*, 50, 693–695.

Leff, J. (1996) Working with families of schizophrenic patients: effects on clinical and social outcomes. In Moscarelli, M., Rupp, A. and Sartorius, N. (eds) *Handbook of Mental Health Economics: Volume I. Schizophrenia*, Wiley, New York, pp. 261–270.

Leff, J. P. and Vaughn, C. E. (1980) The interaction of life events and relatives' expressed emotion in schizophrenia and depressive neurosis, *British Journal of Psychiatry*, 136, 146–153.

Leff, J. and Vaughn, C. (1981) The role of maintenance therapy and relatives' expressed emotion in relapse in schizophrenia, *British Journal of Psychiatry*, 139, 102–104.

Leff, J. and Vaughn, C. (1985) *Expressed Emotion in Families*, Guilford Press, New York.

Lefley, H. P. (1987) Impact of mental illness in families of mental health professionals, *Journal of Nervous and Mental Disease*, 175, 613–619.

Lemkau, P. V. and Crocetti, G. M. (1962) An urban population's opinions and knowledge about mental illness, *American Journal of Psychiatry*, 118, 692–700.

Lidz, T., Fleck, S. and Cornelison, A. (1965) *Schizophrenia and the Family*, International Universities Press, New York.

Link, B. G., Cullen, F. T., Frank, J., *et al.* (1987) The social rejection of former mental patients: understanding why labels matter, *American Journal of Sociology*, 92, 1461–1500.

Link, B. G., Struening, E., Rahav, M., *et al.* (1997) On stigma and its consequences: evidence from a longitudinal study of dual diagnoses of mental illness and substance abuse, *Journal of Health and Social Behavior*, 38, 177–190.

Linszen, D. H., Dingemans, P. M. and Lenior, M. E. (1994) Cannabis abuse and the course of recent-onset schizophrenic disorders, *Archives of General Psychiatry*, 51, 273–279.

Lopez-Ibor, J. J. (1999) Personal communication.

Lysaker, P. and Bell, M. (1995) Work performance over time for people with schizophrenia, *Psychosocial Rehabilitation Journal*, 18, 141–145.

McCreadie, R. G. and Kelly, C. (2000) Patients with schizophrenia who smoke: private disaster, public resource, *British Psychiatry*, 176, 109.

McFarlane, W. R. (ed.) (1983) *Family Therapy in Schizophrenia*, Guilford Press, New York.

McFarlane, W. R., Stastny, P. and Beakins, S. (1992) Family aided assertive community treatment: a comprehensive rehabilitation and intensive case management approach for persons with schizophrenic disorders, *New Directions in Mental Health Services*, 53, 43–54.

MacGregor, S. N., Keith, L. G., Bachicha, J. A., *et al.* (1989) Cocaine abuse during pregnancy: correlation between prenatal care and perinatal outcome, *American Journal of Obstetrics and Gynecology*, 74, 882–885.

McNeil, T. F. (1988) Obstetric factors and perinatal injuries. In Tsuang, M. T. and Simpson, J. C. (eds) *Handbook of Schizophrenia: Nosology, Epidemiology and Genetics*, Elsevier Publishers, New York.

McNeil, T. F., Cantor-Graae, E. and Weinberger, D. R. (2000) Relationship of obstetric complications and differences in size of brain structures in monozygotic twin pairs discordant for schizophrenia, *American Journal of Psychiatry*, 157, 203–212.

Maddi, S. (1981) The existential neurosis, *Journal of Abnormal Psychology*, 72, 311–325.

Madianos, M., Economou, M., Hatjiandreou, M., *et al.* (in press) Changes in public attitudes towards mental illness in the Athens region (1979/1980–1994), *Acta Psychiatrica Scandinavica*.

Malleson, N. (1971) Acute adverse reactions to LSD in clinical and experimental use in the United Kingdom, *British Journal of Psychiatry*, 118, 229–230.

Mandiberg, M. (1999) The sword of reform has two sharp edges: normalcy, normalization, and the destruction of the social group, *New Directions for Mental Health Services*, 83, 31–44.

Manis, M., Houts, P. S. and Blake, J. B. (1963) Beliefs about mental illness as a function of psychiatric status and psychiatric hospitalization, *Journal of Abnormal and Social Psychology*, 67, 226–233.

Marcelis, M., van Os, J., Sham, P., *et al.* (1998) Obstetric complications and familial morbid risk of psychiatric disorders, *American Journal of Medical Genetics*, 81, 29–36.

Marinoni, A., Boidi, G., Botto, G., *et al.* (1996) Prezentazione dei primi dati di follow-up a 5 anni della ricerca sulla schizofrenia in Liguria. Presented at *Il Decorso della Schizofrenia: Studi sul Follow-up*, Genoa, Italy, June 6.

Market and Opinion Research International (1997) *Attitudes Towards Schizophrenia: A Survey of Public Opinions*. Study conducted for Fleishman Hillard Eli Lilly, September.

Markowitz, F. E. (1998) The effects of stigma on the psychological well-being and life satisfaction of persons with mental illness, *Journal of Health and Social Behavior*, 39, 335–347.

Masterson, E. and O'Shea, B. (1984) Smoking and malignancy in schizophrenia, *British Journal of Psychiatry*, 145, 429–432.

Mattson, M. R. and Sacks, M. H. (1983) Seclusion: uses and complications, *American Journal of Psychiatry*, 135, 1210–1213.

Mehta, S. I. and Farina, A. (1988) Associative stigma: perceptions of the difficulties of college-aged children of stigmatized fathers, *Journal of Social and Clinical Psychology*, 7, 192–202.

Meisel, J., McGowan, M., Patotzka, D. and Madison, K. (1993) *Evaluation of AB 3777 Client and Cost Outcomes: July 1990 through March 1992*. California Department of Mental Health, Sacramento, Calif.

Meltzer, H. Y. and Stahl, S. M. (1976) The dopamine hypothesis of schizophrenia: a review, *Schizophrenia Bulletin*, 2, 19–76.

Merzel, C. (1991) Rethinking empowerment, *Health/PAC Bulletin*, Winter, 5–6.

Meyer, J. K. (1964) Attitudes toward mental illness in a Maryland community, *Public Health Reports*, 79, 769–772.

Miller, D. and Dawson, W. H. (1965) Effects of stigma on re-employment of ex-mental patients, *Mental Hygiene*, 49, 281–287.

Moffit, R. (1990) The econometrics of kinked budget constraints, *Journal of Economic Perspectives*, 4, 119–139.

Monahan, J. and Arnold, J. (1996) Violence by people with mental illness: a consensus statement by advocates and researchers, *Psychiatric Rehabilitation Journal*, 19, 67–70.

Mosher, L. R. (1995) The Soteria Project: the first generation American alternatives to psychiatric hospitalization. In Warner, R. (ed.) *Alternatives to Hospital for Acute Psychiatric Treatment*, American Psychiatric Press, Washington, DC, pp. 111–129.

Mosher, L. and Burti, L. (1989) *Community Mental Health: Principles and Practice*, Norton, New York.

Mueser, K. T., Yarnold, P. R., Levinson, D. F., *et al.* (1990) Prevalence of substance abuse in schizophrenia: demographic and clinical correlates, *Schizophrenia Bulletin*, 16, 31–56.

Mueser, K. T., Bond, G. R., Drake, R. E., *et al.* (1998) Models of community care for severe mental illness: a review of research on case management, *Schizophrenia Bulletin*, 24, 37–74.

Mueser, K. T., Yarnold, P. R., Rosenberg, S. D., *et al.* (in press) Substance use disorder in hospitalized severely mentally ill psychiatric patients: prevalence, correlates, and subgroups, *Schizophrenia Bulletin*.

Nestoros, J. N. (1980) Benzodiazepines in schizophrenia: a need for a reassessment, *International Pharmacopsychiatry*, 15, 171–179.

Neugeboren, J. (1997) *Imagining Robert: My Brother, Madness, and Survival*, William Morrow, New York.

Noordsy, D. L., Schwab, B., Fox, L., *et al.* (1996) The role of self-help programs in the rehabilitation of persons with severe mental illness and substance use disorders, *Community Mental Health Journal*, 32, 71–81.

Nunally, J. C. (1961) *Popular Conceptions of Mental Health: Their Development and Change*, Holt, Rinehart & Winston, New York.

Office of National Statistics (1995) *Labour Force Survey*. Office of National Statistics, London.

O'Grady, T. J. (1996) Public attitudes to mental illness, *British Journal of Psychiatry*, 168, 652.

Olmsted, D. W. and Durham, K. (1976) Stability of mental health attitudes: a semantic differential study, *Journal of Health and Social Behavior*, 17, 35–44.

Page, S. (1977) Effects of the mental illness label in attempts to obtain accommodation, *Canadian Journal of Behavioural Science*, 9, 85–90.

Page, S. (1980) Social responsiveness toward mental patients: the general public and others, *Canadian Journal of Psychiatry*, 25, 242–246.

Pai, S. and Kapur, R. L. (1983) Evaluation of home care treatment for schizophrenic patients, *Acta Psychiatrica Scandinavica*, 67, 80–88.

Parashos, J. (1998) *Athenians' Views on Mental and Physical Illness*, Lundbeck Hellas, Athens.

Parker, G. and Hadzi-Pavlovic, D. (1990) Expressed emotion as a predictor of schizophrenic relapse: an analysis of aggregated data, *Psychological Medicine*, 20, 961–965.

Paul, G. L., Tobias, L. L. and Holly, B. L. (1972) Maintenance psychotropic drugs in the presence of active treatment programs: a "triple blind" withdrawal study with long-term mental patients, *Archives of General Psychiatry*, 27, 106–115.

Paykel, E. S., Tylee, A., Wright, A., *et al.* (1997) The Defeat Depression Campaign: psychiatry in the public arena, *American Journal of Psychiatry*, 154, suppl. 6, 59–65.

Paykel, E. S., Hart, D. and Priest, R. G. (1998) Changes in public attitudes to depression during the Defeat Depression Campaign, *British Journal of Psychiatry*, 173, 519–522.

Penn, D. L. and Martin, J. (1998) The stigma of severe mental illness: some potential solutions for a recalcitrant problem, *Psychiatric Quarterly*, 69, 235–247.

Penn, D. L., Guynan, K., Daily, T., *et al.* (1994) Dispelling the stigma of schizophrenia: what sort of information is best? *Schizophrenia Bulletin*, 20, 567–578.

Phelan, J. C., Bromet, E. J. and Link, B. G. (1988) Psychiatric illness and family stigma, *Schizophrenia Bulletin*, 24, 115–126.

Phillips, D. L. (1966) Public identification and acceptance of the mentally ill, *American Journal of Public Health*, 56, 755–763.

Philo, G. (1994) Media images and popular beliefs, *Psychiatric Bulletin*, 18, 173–174.

Piccione, S. (1999) Carico familiare del paziente con diagnosi di schizofrenia: confronto Italia-Usa e review della letteratura. Unpublished dissertation, Department of Psychology, University of Bologna, Bologna, Italy.

Polak, P. and Warner, R. (1996) The economic life of seriously mentally ill people in the community, *Psychiatric Services*, 47, 270–274.

Polak, P. R., Kirby, M. W. and Deitchman, W. S. (1995) Treating acutely ill psychotic patients in private homes. In Warner, R. (ed.) *Alternatives to Hospital for Acute Psychiatric Treatment*, American Psychiatric Press, Washington, DC, pp. 213–223.

Prabhu, G. C., Raghuram, A., Verma, N., *et al.* (1984) Public attitudes toward mental illness: a review, *NIMHANS Journal*, 2, 1–14.

Provencher, H. L. and Mueser, K. T. (1997) Positive and negative symptom behaviors and caregiver burden in the relatives of persons with schizophrenia, *Schizophrenia Research*, 26, 71–80.

Quadagno, J. S. and Antonio, R. J. (1975) Labeling theory as an over-socialized conception of man: the case of mental illness, *Sociology and Social Research*, 60, 33–45.

Rabkin, J. G. (1980) Determinants of public attitudes about mental illness: summary of the research literature. Presented at the National Institute of Mental Health Conference on Stigma Toward the Mentally Ill, Rockville, MD., January, 24–25.

Rabkin, J. G. (1982) Stress and psychiatric disorders. In Goldberger, L. and Breznitz, S. (eds) *Handbook of Stress: Theoretical and Clinical Aspects*, Free Press, New York, pp. 566–584.

Racine, A., Joyce, T. and Anderson, R. (1993) The association between prenatal care and birth weight among women exposed to cocaine in New York City, *Journal of the American Medical Association*, 270, 1581–1586.

Read, J. and Baker, S. (1996) *Not Just Sticks and Stones: A Survey of the Stigma, Taboos and Discrimination Experienced by People with Mental Health Problems*, Mind, London.

Reda, S. (1995) Attitudes towards community mental health care of residents in north London, *Psychiatric Bulletin*, 19, 731–733.

Regier, D. A., Farmer, M. E., Rae, D. S., *et al.* (1990) Comorbidity of mental disorders and alcohol and other drug use: results from the Epidemiologic Catchment Area (ECA) study, *Journal of the American Medical Association*, 264, 2511–2518.

Reinhard, S. C. (1994) Living with mental illness: effects of professional support and personal control on caregiver burden, *Research in Nursing and Health*, 17, 79–88.

Repper, J., Sayce, L., Strong, S., *et al.* (1997) *Tall Stories from the Backyard: A Survey of "Nimby" Opposition to Community Mental Health Facilities, Experienced by Key Service Providers in England and Wales*, Mind, London.

Rice, D. P. and Miller, L. S. (1996) The economic burden of schizophrenia: conceptual and methodological issues, and cost estimates. In Moscarelli, M., Rupp, A. and Sartorius, N. (eds) *Handbook of Mental Health Economics: Volume I. Schizophrenia*, Wiley, New York, pp. 321–334.

Rin, H. and Lin, T. (1962) Mental illness among Formosan aborigines as compared with the Chinese in Taiwan, *Journal of Mental Science*, 108, 134–146.

Robert Wood Johnson Foundation (1990) *Public Attitudes Toward People with Chronic Mental Illness*, The Robert Wood Johnson Foundation Program on Chronic Mental Illness, New Jersey.

Roberts, J. D. and Ward, I. M. (1987) *Commensurate Wage Determination for Service Contracts*, Ohio Industries for the Handicapped, Columbus, Ohio.

Robinson, J. P. and Shaver, P. R. (1969) *Measures of Social Psychological Attitudes*, Institute for Social Research, Ann Arbor, Mich.

Rogers, E. M. (1995) *Diffusion of Innovations*, Free Press, New York.

Rogers, E. M. (1996) The field of health communication today: an up-to-date report, *Journal of Health Communication*, 1, 15–23.

Rogers, E. M., Dearing, J. H., Rao, N., *et al.* (1995) Communication and community in a city under siege: the AIDS epidemic in San Francisco, *Communication Research*, 22, 664–677.

Rogers, E. S., Sciarappa, K., MacDonald-Wilson, K. and Danley, K. (1995) A benefit-cost analysis of a supported employment model for persons with psychiatric disabilities, *Evaluation and Program Planning*, 18, 105–115.

Rosenhan, D. L. (1973) On being sane in insane places, *Science*, 179, 250–258.

Sacker, A., Done, D. J. and Crow, T. J. (1996) Obstetric complications in children born to parents with schizophrenia: a meta-analysis of case-control studies, *Psychological Medicine*, 26, 279–287.

Safer, D. J. (1985) Substance abuse by young adult chronic patients, *Hospital and Community Psychiatry*, 38, 853–858.

Sartorius, N. (1997) Fighting schizophrenia and its stigma: a new World Psychiatric Association educational programme, *British Journal of Psychiatry*, 170, 297.

Sathyavathi, K., Dwarki, B. R. and Murthy, H. N. (1971) Conceptions of mental health, *Transactions of All India Institute of Mental Health*, 11, 37–49.

Sayce, L. (1998) Stigma, discrimination and social exclusion: what's in a word? *Journal of Mental Health*, 7, 331–343.

Scazufca, M. and Kuipers, E. (1996) Links between expressed emotion and burden of care in relatives of patients with schizophrenia, *British Journal of Psychiatry*, 168, 580–587.

Scheff, T. J. (1966) *Being Mentally Ill: A Sociological Theory*, Aldine, Chicago.

Scheper-Hughes, N. (1979) *Saints, Scholars and Schizophrenics: Mental Illness in Rural Ireland*, University of California Press, Berkeley.

Schneier, F. R. and Siris, S. G. (1987) A review of psychoactive substance use and abuse in schizophrenia: patterns of drug choice, *Journal of Nervous and Mental Disease*, 175, 641–652.

Schony, W. (1999) Personal communication.

Sedgwick, P. (1982) *Psycho Politics*, Harper & Row, New York.

Shain, R. E. and Phillips, J. (1991) The stigma of mental illness: labeling and stereotyping in the news. In Wilkins, L. and Patterson, P. (eds) *Risky Business: Communicating Issues of Science, Risk and Public Policy*, Greenwood Press, Westport, Conn.

Sham, P. C., O'Callaghan, E., Takei, N., *et al.* (1992) Schizophrenia following pre-natal exposure to influenza epidemics between 1939 and 1960, *British Journal of Psychiatry*, 160, 461–466.

Sherman, P. S. and Porter, R. (1991) Mental health consumers as case manager aides, *Hospital & Community Psychiatry*, 42, 494–498.

Silvestri, F. (1997) Personal communication.

Sladen-Dew, N., Young, A. M., Parfitt, H., *et al.* (1995) Short-term acute psychiatric treatment in the community: the Vancouver experience. In Warner, R. (ed.) *Alternatives to Hospital for Acute Psychiatric Treatment*, American Psychiatric Press, Washington, DC, pp. 21–34.

Sologg, P. H. (1978) Behavioral precipitants of restraint in the modern milieu, *Comprehensive Psychiatry*, 19, 179–184.

Star, S. (1955) The public's idea about mental illness. Presented at the National Association for Mental Health meeting, Chicago, Ill., November.

Steadman, H. and Cocozza, J. (1978) Selective reporting and the public's misconceptions of the criminally insane, *Public Opinion Quarterly*, 41, 523–533.

Stein, L. I. and Test, M. A. (1980) Alternative to mental hospital treatment: I. Conceptual model, treatment program, and clinical evaluation, *Archives of General Psychiatry*, 37, 392–397.

Strauss, J. S. and Carpenter, W. T. (1981) *Schizophrenia*, Plenum, New York.

Sturgeon, D., Kuipers, L., Berkowitz, R., *et al.* (1981) Psychophysiological responses of schizophrenic patients to high and low expressed emotion relatives, *British Journal of Psychiatry*, 138, 40–45.

Suddath, R. L., Christison, G. W., Torrey, E. F., *et al.* (1990) Anatomical abnormalities in the brains of monozygotic twins discordant for schizophrenia, *New England Journal of Schizophrenia*, 322, 789–794.

Surles, R. C., Morrison, B. J., Sheets, J. L., *et al.* (1992) *Buy OMH Directory of Products and Services*. New York State Office of Mental Health Bureau of Psychiatric Rehabilitation Services, Albany, NY.

Swanson, R. M. and Spitzer, S. P. (1970) Stigma and the psychiatric patient career, *Journal of Health and Social Behavior*, 11, 44–51.

Swartz, M. S., Swanson, J. W., Wagner, H. R., *et al.* (1999) Can involuntary out-patient commitment reduce hospital recidivism? Findings from a randomized trial with severely mentally ill individuals, *American Journal of Psychiatry*, 156, 1968–1975.

Tamminga, C. A., Thaker, G. K., Buchanan, R., *et al.* (1992) Limbic system abnormalities identified in schizophrenia using positron emission tomography with fluorodeoxyglucose and neocortical alterations with deficit syndrome, *Archives of General Psychiatry*, 49, 522–530.

Tarrier, N., Vaughn, C. E., Lader, M. H., *et al.* (1979) Bodily reaction to people and events in schizophrenics, *Archives of General Psychiatry*, 36, 311–315.

Tarrier, N., Beckett, R., Harwood, S., *et al.* (1993) A trial of two cognitive-behavioural methods of treating drug-resistant residual psychotic symptoms in schizophrenic patients: I. Outcome, *British Journal of Psychiatry*, 162, 524–532.

Tarrier, N., Wittowski, A., Kinney, C., *et al.* (1999) Durability of the effects of cognitive-behavioural therapy in the treatment of chronic schizophrenia 12-month follow-up, *British Journal of Psychiatry*, 174, 500–504.

Taylor, D. and Warner, R. (1994) Does substance use precipitate the onset of functional psychosis? *Social Work and Social Sciences Review*, 5, 64–75.

Telintelo, S., Kuhlman, T. L. and Winget, C. (1983) A study of the use of restraint in a psychiatric emergency room, *Hospital and Community Psychiatry*, 34, 164–165.

Tennent, F. S. and Groesbeck, C. J. (1972) Psychiatric effects of hashish, *Archives of General Psychiatry*, 27, 133–136.

Terry, P. B., Condie, R. G., Bissenden, J. G. and Keridge, D. F. (1987) Ethnic differences in incidence of very low birth weight and neonatal deaths among normally formed infants, *Archives of Disease of Childhood*, 62, 709–711.

Test, M. A., Wallisch, L. S., Allness, D. J., *et al.* (1989) Substance use in young adults with schizophrenic disorders, *Schizophrenia Bulletin*, 15, 465–476.

Thompson, E. H. and Doll, W. (1982) The burden of families coping with the mentally ill: an invisible crisis, *Family Relations*, 31, 379–388.

Tringo, J. L. (1970) The hierarchy of preference towards disability groups, *Journal of Special Education*, 4, 295–306.

Trute, B. and Segal, S. P. (1976) Census tract predictors and the social integration of sheltered care residents, *Social Psychiatry*, 11, 153–161.

Vaughn, C. E. and Leff, J. P. (1976) The influence of family and social factors on the course of psychiatric illness: a comparison of schizophrenic and depressed neurotic patients, *British Journal of Psychiatry*, 129, 125–137.

Verghese, A. and Beig, A. (1974) Public attitude towards mental illness: the Vellore study, *Indian Journal of Psychiatry*, 16, 8–18.

Wadeson, J. and Carpenter, W. T. (1976) The impact of the seclusion room experience, *Journal of Nervous and Mental Disease*, 163, 318–328.

Wahl, O. F. (1995) *Media Madness: Public Images of Mental Illness*, Rutgers University Press, New Brunswick, NJ.

Wang, S., Sun, C., Walczak, C. A., *et al.* (1995) Evidence for a susceptibility locus for schizophrenia on chromosome 6pter-p22, *Nature Genetics*, 10, 41–46.

Warner, R. (1994) *Recovery from Schizophrenia: Psychiatry and Political Economy*, Routledge, New York.

Warner, R. (1995) From patient management to risk management. In R. Warner (ed.) *Alternatives to the Hospital for Acute Psychiatric Treatment*, American Psychiatric Press, Washington, D. C., pp. 237–248.

Warner, R. (ed.) (1995) *Alternatives to the Hospital for Acute Psychiatric Care*, American Psychiatric Press, Washington, DC.

Warner, R. and Atkinson, M. (1988) The relationship between schizophrenic patients' perceptions of their parents and the course of their illness, *British Journal of Psychiatry*, 153, 344–353.

Warner, R. and de Girolamo, G. (1995) *Epidemiology of Mental Problems and Psychosocial Problems: Schizophrenia*, World Health Organization, Geneva.

Warner, R. and Huxley, P. (1993) Psychopathology and quality of life among mentally ill patients in the community: British and US samples compared, *British Journal of Psychiatry*, 163, 505–509.

Warner, R. and Huxley, P. (1998) Outcome for people with schizophrenia before and after Medicaid capitation at a community mental health center in Colorado, *Psychiatric Services*, 49, 802–807.

Warner, R. and Polak, P. (1995) The economic advancement of the mentally ill in the community: economic opportunities, *Community Mental Health Journal*, 31, 381–396.

Warner, R. and Ruggieri, M. (1997) The quality of life of people with schizophrenia in Boulder, Colorado, and Verona, Italy. Unpublished manuscript, Mental Health Center of Boulder County, Boulder, Colo.

Warner, R. and Wollesen, C. (1995) Cedar House: a non-coercive hospital alternative in Boulder, Colorado. In R. Warner (ed.) *Alternatives to Hospital for Acute Psychiatric Treatment*, American Psychiatric Press, Washington, DC, pp. 3–17.

Warner, R., Huxley, P., and Berg, T. (1999) An evaluation of the impact of club-house membership on quality of life and treatment utilization, *International Journal of Social Psychiatry*, 45, 310–321.

Warner, R., Miklowitz, D. and Sachs-Ericsson, N. (1991) Expressed emotion, patient attributes and outcome in psychosis. Presented at the Royal College of Psychiatrists Spring Quarterly Meeting, Leicester, England.

Warner, R., Taylor, D., Powers, M., *et al.* (1989) Acceptance of the mental illness label by psychotic patients: effects on functioning, *American Journal of Orthopsychiatry*, 59, 398–409.

Warner, R., Taylor, D., Wright, J., *et al.* (1994) Substance use among the mentally ill: prevalence, reasons for use and effects on illness, *American Journal of Orthopsychiatry*, 64, 465–476.

Warner, R., de Girolamo, G., Belelli, G., *et al.* (1998) The quality of life of people with schizophrenia in Boulder, Colorado, and Bologna, Italy, *Schizophrenia Bulletin*, 24, 559–568.

Waxler, N. E. (1977) Is mental illness cured in traditional societies? A theoretical analysis, *Culture, Medicine and Psychiatry*, 1, 233–253.

Weinberger, D. R., Berman, K. F., Suddath, R., *et al.* (1992) Evidence of a dysfunction of a prefrontal-limbic network in schizophrenia: a magnetic resonance imaging and regional cerebral blood flow study of discordant monozygotic twins, *American Journal of Psychiatry*, 149, 890–897.

Weiner, B., Perry, R. P. and Magnusson, J. (1988) An attributional analysis of reactions to stigmas, *Journal of Personality and Social Psychology*, 55, 738–748.

Weinstein, R. M. (1983) Labeling theory and the attitudes of mental patients: a review, *Journal of Health and Social Behavior*, 24, 70–84.

Wing, J. K. (1978) The social context of schizophrenia, *American Journal of Psychiatry*, 135, 1333–1339.

Wolff, G. (1997) Attitudes of the media and the public. In J. Leff (ed.) *Care in the Community: Illusion or Reality?* Wiley, New York, pp. 144–163.

World Health Organization (1979) *Schizophrenia: An International Follow-up Study*, Wiley, Chichester, England.

Wykes, T., Parr, A.-M. and Landau, S. (1999) Group treatment of auditory hallucinations: exploratory study of effectiveness, *British Journal of Psychiatry*, 175, 180–185.

Yalom, I. D. (1980) *Existential Psychotherapy*, Basic Books, New York.

Yarrow, M., Clausen, J. and Robbins, P. (1955) The social meaning of mental illness, *Journal of Social Issues*, 11, 33–48.

Yip, K. S. (1998) Personal communication.

Zisook, S., Heaton, R., Moranville, J., *et al.* (1992) Past substance abuse and clinical course of schizophrenia, *American Journal of Psychiatry*, 149, 552–553.

Zornberg, G. L., Buka, S. L. and Tsuang, M. T. (2000) Hypoxic ischaemia-related fetal/neonatal complications and risk of schizophrenia and other nonaffective psychoses: a 19-year longitudinal study, *American Journal of Psychiatry*, 157, 196–202.

Zuckerman, B., Frank, D. A., Hingson, R., *et al.* (1989) Effects of maternal marijuana and cocaine use on fetal growth, *New England Journal of Medicine*, 320, 762–768.

Index